California
Blue Ribbon Trout Streams

Brad Jackson

Bill Sunderland and Dale Lackey

Frank Amato
PORTLAND

10 9 8 7 6 5 4 3 2

Copyright 1991 • Dale Lackey/Bill Sunderland • Printed in Singapore
Book Design: Joyce Herbst • Typesetting: Charlie Clifford
Front Cover Photo: Brad Jackson • Back Cover Photo: Dale Lackey • Maps: Tony Amato
Soft Bound: ISBN 1-878175-00-9 • Hard Bound: ISBN 1-878175-01-7

CONTENTS

Brad Jackson

INTRODUCTION

California offers fine trout fishing, partly because it has such a varied geography. There are the goldens in High Sierra lakes, mackinaws in Lake Tahoe, and rainbows, browns, brookies and cutthroats in the myriad streams, rivers, lakes and reservoirs that are everywhere.

That's the problem—there is such a smorgasbord of good trout fishing in Northern California that anglers often have trouble deciding where to go and how to fish an area when they get there.

Some spots are well known: Hat Creek, McCloud River, Fall River, Eagle Lake, the Upper Sacramento. But what about such jewels as Heenan Lake, the Kings River, the East Carson River and Pleasant Valley?

That's what this book is about, where to go and the best fishing methods to use when you get there. There isn't enough room in one book to offer details of every trout fishing area in California—such a book would look like the Los Angeles Yellow Pages. Instead, we have chosen a variety of localities that stretch from the Owens River near Mammoth Lakes on the Eastern Sierra slope to the Upper Sacramento near the Oregon border. We believe these regions contain most of the best fishing in the state.

We have selected areas that you can get to by car, with only an occasional spot where four-wheel drive is necessary. Some are well known and an angler almost certainly will have company fishing there. Others, despite this drive-up ability, give those who prefer to fish alone an opportunity to do so, particularly if they are willing to hike up or down stream. We've noted that within easy hiking distance, several miles at the most, there may be a lake or stream you might want to try. But we have stayed away from the day-long hike that often is necessary to reach some of the prime High Sierra lakes.

In addition to our first-hand knowledge of the rivers,

Don Vachini

streams and lakes, we quote the "experts"—guides, sporting goods shop owners and employees, and locals who have fished there day in and day out, year after year. This has paid off with the best of inside information, the kind of angling know-how it takes years to learn.

Each chapter covers a specific area that can be fished as a "destination package." Generally, it is a drainage area, but in some chapters, such as the one on the Upper Sacramento, the river itself is so long and varied that it alone remains the focus.

The book is designed for use by fly fishermen and by bait and spin anglers. It tells which fly patterns are best, and what lures or bait the locals depend on. In most cases, more detail is provided for the fly fisherman since the type and size of flies can be important and varied, while a limited variety of bait and lures are used for trout fishing.

Most important, we describe accurately and honestly what to expect when you fish an area. If there are no big fish, then you'll know before driving 250 miles that 10-inch brookies are the best you can catch. Or, if your prime objective is to get your limit each day, we detail sections where there are regular plants by the state Department of Fish and Game and the chances are good for filling your creel.

Of course there are regulations for every stream. Where they are special, such as catch and release, fly fishing only, or a size and bag limit differs from the general regulations, we have noted them. But regulations change, so please check the DFG's regulations pamphlet, which is available free at most sporting goods or bait and tackle shops. An easy way is to get one when you buy your fishing license for the year and then keep it with the gear you always use.

We are not addressing in great detail the question of what gear to use. This isn't a "how to" book, but is for the angler looking for a reference work on where there is the best trout fishing in California.

We also hope it is for the angler who truly enjoys fishing for the sake of the sport, the man or woman who plays by the rules and happily returns a wild trout to the stream or lake to live and fight again another day. If you love to fish, you'll want to share the joy with those who follow you.

Catch and release has become a key to conservation in California. If anglers do not release wild trout then there soon will be none left. Think of fishing only for hatchery-bred trout. No more of those small stream brookies, only a few lunker browns, no High Sierra goldens, an occasional Lahontan cutthroat.

There is certainly nothing wrong with taking a limit of planted rainbows. Their chances of living into the next season is small anyway and, to be blunt, that's why the Department of Fish and Game puts millions of them into California streams each year.

But only rarely is that brookie, brown or cutthroat caught away from easy-access areas planted. Life is tougher there and only the fighters survive. Put them back to fight again.

Using barbless hooks helps. And despite the common misconception, only occasionally is a fish lost because the hook had a pressed-down barb. For fly fishermen there's a more selfish reason—a barbless hook in the ear is a lot easier to get out and may not require a trip to the nearest emergency room.

If you are going to put a fish back, don't play it long. Studies have shown that some trout caught and released die anyway because they were played to exhaustion or handled roughly before being returned to the water. Never touch a fish's gills, and if possible hold them in slow water while removing the hook. Don't just toss them back in—hold them gently facing upstream, moving them backward and forward to allow water to flow through their gills, until they are strong enough to swim quickly away from your hands.

We hope we are trying to convert anglers who already are true believers, but a bit more preaching can't hurt.

Our theory of fishing, such as it is, doesn't run to the "bigger is better" school of thought. Catching big trout is fun, but a day of flipping dry flies to eight- and 10-inch brookies is just as exciting. And hooking a 12-inch brown from a clear mountain creek where you think there is nothing but small rainbows, particularly on a light-weight rod, is as much fun as tying into a 20-incher in a trophy trout area.

Part of the trout fishing experience is where it takes place. You don't find trout in polluted, luke-warm streams. They're shy creatures demanding the purest of water. They live in areas such as the Trinity Alps, the Sierra, or Sequoia National Forest. What a combination—bliss indeed!

Be sure and preserve both the trout fishing and the natural beauty for your grandchildren.

Bill Sunderland

7

Chapter One

BAIT AND LURE FISHING

—DALE LACKEY

The most popular lures for trout are spinners and spoons. Spinners have a main body, usually made of metal, that often is simply a wire strung with colored beads. When retrieved, the blade spins around the body.

Heavy spinners, such as Panther Martins, are designed to be cast and retrieved. Others have a light body made of beads and paper-thin blades and can be cast and retrieved or drift-fished to roll along the bottom in moving water.

Spoons are stamped from a single piece of metal with a concave or twisted shape to make them wiggle as they are retrieved. Spoons can be trolled, or cast and retrieved. Plugs such as Rapalas imitate bait fish and are either cast and retrieved or trolled behind a boat.

When fishing a stream with a spoon or a spinner, be sure to tie a snap swivel on the end of the line to keep it from being twisted by the lure as it spins. And add enough weight to get the lure to the bottom of the stream.

In moving water, cast the lure upstream and let it sink to near the bottom. The pressure of the current against the line will carry it downstream and make the blades flash. The blades do not have to spin fast to catch fish.

The lure also can be cast across the stream. As soon as it hits the water, tighten the line and let it swing across the current in an arc. If it begins to sink in slow current, retrieve just fast enough to keep it off the bottom.

A third technique is to cast the lure upstream to the head of a deep pool, let it sink, then retrieve it quickly past the head of the pool, which is an excellent holding area for trout.

One other way to fish a spinner in a stream is to suspend it below a sliding bobber. Adjust the bobber depth so the spinner barely clears or lightly drags along the bottom. Spinners with very light blades are best for this. Select a spot where you

Brad Jackson

feel the fish are holding and cast above it. Make sure you cast far enough upstream to allow the spinner to sink. Watch the bobber carefully for any hesitation. This works better in turbulent water than in calm pools.

The final technique is to troll it behind a boat. Use enough weight to keep the lure under the surface and down to the level where the fish are holding. The problem obviously is to find out hwere the fish are, and experimenting at different depths often is the only way.

The most common mistake made by trollers is going too fast. To determine the proper speed, lower the lure just below the surface alongside the boat and adjust the boat speed until the lure resembles a fish moving through the water. A spoon should swing back and forth, and the blades of a spinner should move slowly enough that you can see them as they spin.

Whenever you use any kind of lure, cast to a specific area, especially if you are moving through in a boat. Several years ago while guiding for steelhead on the Klamath River, we spent most of the day casting and retrieving Panther Martins. I was hooking more than half the fish we caught although I was fishing less than 10 percent of the time. I began watching to see what I did that was different from my guests.

As the boat drifted downstream, I would cast only to likely fish holding areas. My guests used the shotgun approach, casting and retrieving, then casting again. I began pointing to spots for them to cast to, and told them not to cast unless it was into a good looking area. The shotgun approach left them unprepared as we passed good spots, rocks and eddies, because most of the time their lines were already in the water.

As they began to conserve their casts, the number of fish they caught went way up. In fact, they were casting into the areas they had been leaving for me and I was too busy netting their fish to be able to fish myself.

Bait

Protein in its various forms is the most consistent way to catch fish—night crawlers, grasshoppers, minnows, salmon eggs, crickets, cheese and all of the various concoctions that have come on the market in recent years.

The most common method of fishing bait is to let it soak on the bottom, or to suspend it off the bottom with a bobber. But that works only if fish are moving through an area or if they are milling around in a pool.

Most of the time, you'll do better by taking the bait to the fish.

Drift fishing is where the bait rolls along the bottom of a stream, carried by the current. About 24 inches above the hook, either tie a barrel swivel into the line and put a sliding sinker on the line above the swivel or crimp a few pieces of split shot onto the monofilament. Either way, be sure to use enough weight to get the bait to the bottom. It is necessary for the bait to sink fast but it must be light enough to allow the current to roll it along the bottom.

It is actually the pressure of the current on the line that carries the rig downstream. You will feel the weight bounce along, hitting rocks, gravel and snags. If the line hesitates for any reason, set the hook—a fish may have picked up the bait. More likely it will be the line hanging up on a snag, but setting the hook is good insurance since you would have to pull it free anyway.

The main drawback of drift fishing is that a lot of gear is lost on the bottom. On the other hand, it is one of the most effective ways to catch big trout.

Many people fishing a quiet pool or lake are content to let a night crawler soak on the bottom. That works if the fish are moving. If they aren't, they'll never find the bait unless it is well placed. Try dragging the bait, especially a night crawler, along the bottom. Retrieve it very slowly a foot or so, then let it rest. Then retrieve again.

Another technique is to fish the bait under a bobber. Set the bobber so the line is a bit shorter than the water depth, thereby keeping the bait just off the bottom. If fishing a stream, cast it up and let it come down with the current. If fishing a lake, start deep and gradually set it shallower until you find the depth the fish are holding.

Hook live minnows behind the dorsal fin so they can swim around. Dead minnows are hooked through the lips. Thread a night crawler on a worm threader and slide it over the hook and up the line.

Salmon eggs or Power Bait can be pushed on the hook. Just remember to use a small enough hook so that the bait will hide almost all of it.

If you feel you've covered a pool and nothing is happening, move on. You can always come back later.

There is one common denominator among anglers who catch lots of fish—they fish every cast as though they believe it is going to catch a fish. That's EVERY cast. When they no longer feel that way, they rest for a while then continue fishing when they feel better.

The bottom line is this: fish every instant of every cast as though the biggest fish of your life is about to hit. When it does, you will be ready.

Autumn colors on the Fall River. Frank Raymond

Chapter Two

FLY FISHING—BILL SUNDERLAND

There's no mystery to fly fishing; like most other sports it just takes a bit of patience and practice to get it right.

It is well worth the time. I've done most types of fishing, both salt water and fresh water, and the sensation of working a fly on a Sierra creek is as good as it gets. There's a deep, personal satisfaction from overcoming currents, stream-side shrubbery and all the other impediments to attain a drag-free float that brings a rainbow or a brookie slamming to the surface after that tiny piece of fur and feathers. It is a step above what I've ever achieved with lures or bait.

If I'm preaching to the converted, your time is better spent fishing. However, if you are an angler who has considered trying fly fishing but never got around to it or were unsure how to start, maybe this will help.

Fly fishing, more than most other types of angling, can be an expensive hobby—graphite/boron rods, milled aluminum reels, a dozen different fly lines, neoprene waders, a vest laden with 15 pounds of gadgets that may be used once in a lifetime, and an entomological encyclopedia of flies that cost from $1.25 to $2 apiece and mostly end up in trees 12 feet above the water line.

"There goes $2,000 on the hoof," is the caustic comment of many a bait-slinger watching a fully-outfitted flyfisherman. There's a lot of truth to that remark. The other side of the coin is simple: Buying fly fishing gear can be fun, particularly if you are one of the lucky ones who can afford it.

Fun, but certainly not necessary.

What you do need to start with are a rod, reel and fly line. Several companies, including Orvis and Cortland, make packages which include all three for around $100. That's probably as cheap as it is going to get, less than you'll spend buying the gear separately. It is important,

Brad Jackson

however, that you know what you are getting, so here is some detail on basic equipment.

Rods: A good graphite rod costs around $300. Rods that are fine for a beginning fly angler are available for less than $100.

Since casting is the key to fly fishing, buying a cheap rod will make learning that much more difficult because most of them cast like car antennas. Stick with graphite— fiberglass is outdated and bamboo is out of sight. If you are lucky enough to have inherited a couple of grandpa's bamboo rods, leave them in the closet until you know what you are doing. Even then, you may end up selling them to buy good graphite rods.

Rods come in different lengths and weights. The weight refers to the line it is designed to cast, with #1 being the lightest and #12 about the heaviest. Very light rods (#3 and below) are nearly impossible to cast in any breeze, or for any distance, and the heaviest rods (#10 and up) are designed for fighting marlin, sailfish and other big saltwater species. An all-purpose rod that can be used any place from a creek to a good-sized river is a #6, so try to find something in that range.

The weight of line fly fishing rods are designed to cast is marked on them, generally near the logo of the maker. As to length, stick to the all-purpose range of 8 or 9 feet. Using a fly rod isn't like flipping a lure with a 6-foot boat rod; you need some backbone.

Lines: You must match the line to the rod. In other words, if you buy a #6 weight rod you need a #6 weight line to go with it. There is a variety of lines on the market and you should know some basics before deciding what to buy. First, some lines are designed to float and others are designed to sink. Sinking lines come in a number of densities that make them sink at different rates. Other lines are made to float except for the final 10 feet or so and are called sink-tip lines. To start, get a cheap floating line. Since you need to practice, often on lawn or pavement when no water is available, it'll take a beating.

Even floating lines come in different types, mostly designed to help casting. A level line is just that—the entire line, usually about 70 to 80 feet, has no taper. Few of these are left, and you don't want one anyway.

Generally, lines are marked "weight forward." This is designed to make them easier to cast since it is the weight of the line that carries the fly to its destination, unlike spin casting where the line has almost no weight and the lure is the projectile carrying the line with it.

There are any number of expensive lines on the market. Each one claims to provide the ultimate in casting and most of them have something to offer. But until you are pretty well versed in handling a flyline they aren't going to do you enough good to make the investment worthwhile. So on your first go-around buy a cheap line. By the time you graduate to the advanced class you'll have worn the line out anyway.

Once you start fly fishing regularly you'll also need a sinking line. Sinking lines are denser (so they will break the film of the water and sink) and as a result are harder to cast. In addition, retrieving a sinking line from under water for a cast is more difficult than pulling a line off the top of the water.

A good second line is a sink-tip line. The first 10 feet are dense enough to sink, the rest of the line is floating line. This won't work when you really need to get deep, but it is an all-purpose line that is a part of every fly fisherman's collection. You don't need to buy it on the first go-around, but keep it in mind for someplace down the road.

The type of line is shown on the package. Most companies also include a sticker someplace in the package that can be peeled off and put on the spool of the reel. When you collect a half-dozen spools with different types of line on them it becomes crucial to know what each line is.

Here's a key to some common designations of lines:
WF6F—Weight forward, #6 weight, floating.
WF7F/S—Weight forward, #7 weight, floating line with a sink tip.
WF8S—Weight forward, #8 weight, sinking.

Reels: The old adage is that a fly reel is just a place to hang the line and doesn't need to be fancy. That's not always true—hooking into a monster fish can tear a cheap reel to pieces—but for your first set of gear it is true enough. Two points you might want to consider, however:

(1) Get a reel for which you can buy extra spools. It's very handy to have that sink-tipped line all wrapped onto a spool, complete with leader and ready to go in your pocket if you are out on a stream and decide to switch lines. Extra spools generally cost about half as much as the complete reel.

(2) If possible, buy a fly reel that you can "palm" to increase the drag. This means the edge of the spool, which is the part that turns with the line, is not protected by the body of the reel. Many reels have a rim built into the body that protects the edge of the spool. While this decreases the possibility of damage to the spool, it means that if you get a big fish and want to put more pressure on it, you can't put your palm gently against the outside edge of the revolving spool to increase the drag.

Most fishing reels have a built-in, adjustable drag, but particularly on the cheaper reels they tend to be rough and hard to manipulate, and wear out easily. If you fish for really big fish you will want to invest in a reel that is tough enough to do the job properly. However, they are expensive and to start you don't need to spend that kind of money.

Mayfly and shuck. Dale Lackey

Leader/Tippet: You can always tie a lure or a hook directly onto a monofilament line, but a fly line must have a leader and tippet. The leader is tapered to the end and a tippet is the additional couple of feet tied onto that. The size of a tippet is a key in your fishing since it is what will break and cost you either a fish or a fly. The two factors of a leader/tippet setup are length and strength. A short leader for dry fly fishing is 7 feet (for underwater nymph fishing leaders are shorter and the tippets stronger). Leaders need to be 15 feet long, sometimes even more, when fishing in clear water for Harvard-educated lunkers.

Just remember that the longer and lighter the leader the tougher it is to cast properly since, like the fly, it has almost no weight and must be carried by the weight of the fly line.

"Turning over" the leader, or the fly line itself, is a common phrase. It means laying out the line and leader during the cast so that from an on-its-side U moving forward it unfolds into a straight, untangled line as it reaches the end of the cast and drops onto the water.

Leaders and tippets come with a designation that indicates their strength. This varies from maker to maker, but for general purposes here's a key:

8X = 1.5 lb. test	3X = 7.5 lb. test
7X = 2.5 lb. test	2X = 9 lb. test
6X = 4 lb. test	1X = 10 lb. test
5X = 5 lb. test	0X = 11 lb. test
4X = 6 lb. test	

Knots: Okay, Boy and Girl Scouts, now is the time to learn your knots. There are a few that you'll use regularly and the time spent practicing them, no matter how frustrating, will be repaid a thousand-fold in time spent fishing. Unless tying a tippet or a fly is automatic, every time you have to change one you'll face a problem. It also means that you won't be changing tippets or flies when you should be because you won't want to face that problem.

Upper falls on the McCloud. Dale Lackey

The leader is attached to the fly line with a needle knot or nail knot, which are about the same thing. They're handy to know, but not crucial if you have a reference diagram when you need it. In fact, most leader packages have a drawing of a needle/nail knot on them.

The tippet and leader go together with a blood knot, and the fly is attached to the tippet with an improved clinch knot. Most fly lines include a pamphlet that shows how to tie these knots.

Once you have everything (and have passed your Scout knot-tying exam), you need to put it together. Start with at least 100 yards of 15 or 20 pound test braided backing on the reel. In addition to acting as a backup if you hook into a big one that takes out all your line, it will make reeling a lot easier.

Fly reels (except for big, expense saltwater reels) are direct drive — you turn the crank once and the reel turns around once. If the line is attached directly to the spool, that means the wraps will be a lot smaller, which in turn means that every time you make a complete turn of the reel you take in less line. The way around that is to use about 100 to 150 yards of backing, which fills up about half of the reel, before you attach the backing to the end of the fly line.

How you put the backing and line on the reel is determined by whether you cast right or left handed. If you hold your rod in your right hand to cast, then you'll reel left handed. Reels are designed to be reeled either way, but you have to put the line on so it is correct for you. You reel overhand, so once the backing is attached to the spool make certain you bring it on to the reel that way.

It's easier to make a mistake doing this than you think, so in the interest of being right the first time attach the reel to the butt of your rod and reel the backing and line onto the gear holding it the same way you would while fishing.

Most fly lines have a built-in loop at the butt end. Use an improved clinch knot or any other small, secure knot to attach the backing to the line. Most fly lines are wound onto the spool on which they are sold so that the butt is on the outside, ready to be attached to the backing.

Once the backing and line are on the spool, attach a leader with a needle or nail knot and you're ready to go.

Fall fishing on the McCloud River. Brad Jackson

A nice brown trout caught on an Elk Caddis. Brad Jackson

But Before You Go Fishing. . .

You need to learn how to use your rod. A couple of hours practice in an open space big enough to give you room for casting will have you handling 30 feet of line with reasonable accuracy. That's all you need to start — more than 80 percent of fly casting is within that range, no matter what your ability.

You might as well learn to cast properly the first time, since it is a learned ability rather than a "natural" action.

Probably the best (and most expensive) way is to take lessons. Fly fishing shops almost always have instructors available. Joining a local fly fishing club, if one is in your area, is excellent. Dues are low and they usually have casting classes sometime during the year. The only problem is that when they are giving classes might not be when you want to learn.

The alternative is books or videotapes. Personally, I'm a reader rather than a watcher, so I prefer books. There are a number of excellent books on casting by Mel Krieger, Doug Swisher and Joan Salvato Wulff, among others. Each offers his or her own technique, and all are excellent. (There are almost as many "right" ways to cast as there are "wrong" ways.)

For watchers, there are videos both by those who have written books and by a number of other well-known fly casters. There's an added advantage — rather than forking out the dough to buy a video you can generally rent them from local fly fishing or sporting goods stores.

And Finally. . .

You'll need a few flies to get started. Buy a couple of what are called attractors — flies that are "buggy" but do not imitate any specific insect. Royal Wulffs or Humpies are fine, size 12 or 14. They'll take care of you just about anywhere. If you are going to fish a specific area, you can always ask the local sporting goods store what the fish are biting on.

Flies are tied by hook size, with the larger the number the smaller the fly. They come in even numbers only — 8, 10, 12, etc. Most dry flies are in size 10 or smaller, all the way up to minuscule size 22s and 24s. Flies tied to imitate larvae or nymphs often are on slightly larger, heavier hooks and are fished underwater rather than floating on the surface.

Five words of caution that should appear on all gear by order of the surgeon general: "WARNING: Fly fishing is addictive!"

Just watch out or pretty soon your old fishing buddies will be sneering at you and commenting to each other, "There goes $2,000 on the hoof."

Chapter Three

UPPER SACRAMENTO RIVER

The Sacramento River generally is considered to start at Big Springs, where the clear, cold water bubbles out of the ground in the city park in the town of Mount Shasta. But the Sacramento really starts as snow on the slopes of Mount Shasta, where the melt becomes small streams that disappear underground, then reappear as myriad springs that dot the valleys surrounding the 14,162-foot-high mountain dominating Northern California.

Dale Lackey

The upper Sacramento, from its headwaters to the huge Shasta Lake backed up behind the dam north of Redding, is a nearly perfect trout stream, popular and productive for lure and bait anglers as well as for fly fishers.

Access along the entire stream is almost unlimited. The Southern Pacific Rail Road tracks follow the Sacramento through the canyon and anglers who don't mind walking the rail bed can fish just about each of the nearly 35 miles of stream from Cantara Loop to Shasta Lake.

Only the stream from below Box Canyon Dam to Cantara Loop can't be accessed from the tracks. But the angler can enter the stream at Ney Springs and work his or her way up to Box Canyon Dam or down to Cantara.

Anglers tend to congregate at the easy-to-reach spots, especially campgrounds and swimming holes. The most popular include Soda Creek, Sims Campground, Dog Creek and Delta.

But they also can avoid crowds by fishing areas that require only a short walk. Access areas are so plentiful that often even a quarter-of-a-mile walk means they will have a piece of the stream to themselves.

Technique

Spinning Gear: Ultra-light spinning gear is ideal for the upper Sacramento. Load a reel with easy-to-cast line, such as Stren or Trilene, and use a six or seven foot light-action rod.

Bait: The great thing about bait is that there really isn't much to choose from. Use #8 or #10 hooks, bought loose in a box. Disregard the packages that are already snelled.

Berkley Power Bait has come on like gang busters in every stream and lake it has been tried on, and the Sacramento is as good a place as any to use it. Or you can go with the old standards such as crickets and salmon eggs, especially Pautzke Fireballs. But no bait has been more consistent on the stream than worms or night crawlers. For most purposes, thread half a crawler over the hook with a worm threader and slide it up the line.

Lures: Small spinners work best, one-eighth or one-quarter ounce Panther Martins, Mepps or Super Dupers, in yellow or red. The experienced angler fishes a spinner just as he would bait. Rather than cast and retrieve (which also works just fine), drift the lure along the bottom of the stream, letting the blades work in the current. This gets down to where the big fish hang out. Cast to the head of a pool, or cast above large boulders and let the spinner swing past them along the edge of the holding areas, or let it follow the edge of the main current, right in the feeding lane of the fish. Work the lure along that line of bubbles at the edge of the current.

Fly Fishing: The name of one man is synonymous with Sacramento River fly fishing—Ted Fay. Fay was a small man with a pair of the largest ears most of us had ever seen. But he certainly knew how to tie a fly, tying more than 10,000 a year for many years.

Fay was known for his "dropper" double fly system. He spliced a short leader about two feet up from the end of

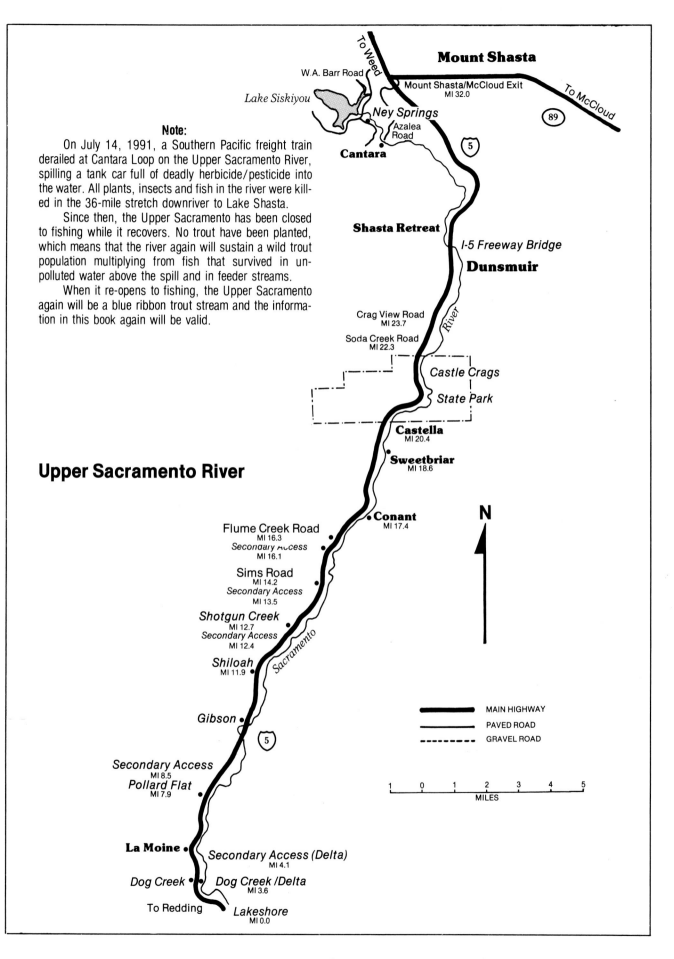

Mount Shasta

To Weed

W.A. Barr Road

Mount Shasta/McCloud Exit
MI 32.0

To McCloud

Lake Siskiyou

89

Ney Springs

Azalea Road

Cantara

5

Note:

On July 14, 1991, a Southern Pacific freight train derailed at Cantara Loop on the Upper Sacramento River, spilling a tank car full of deadly herbicide/pesticide into the water. All plants, insects and fish in the river were killed in the 36-mile stretch downriver to Lake Shasta.

Since then, the Upper Sacramento has been closed to fishing while it recovers. No trout have been planted, which means that the river again will sustain a wild trout population multiplying from fish that survived in unpolluted water above the spill and in feeder streams.

When it re-opens to fishing, the Upper Sacramento again will be a blue ribbon trout stream and the information in this book again will be valid.

Shasta Retreat

I-5 Freeway Bridge

Dunsmuir

River

Crag View Road
MI 23.7

Soda Creek Road
MI 22.3

Castle Crags

State Park

Castella
MI 20.4

• **Sweetbriar**
MI 18.6

Upper Sacramento River

• **Conant**
MI 17.4

N

Flume Creek Road
MI 16.3
Secondary Access
MI 16.1

Sims Road
MI 14.2
Secondary Access
MI 13.5

Shotgun Creek
MI 12.7
Secondary Access
MI 12.4

Shiloah
MI 11.9

Sacramento

Gibson •

5

Secondary Access
MI 8.5
Pollard Flat
MI 7.9 •

| | | | | | | | MAIN HIGHWAY |
| PAVED ROAD |
| GRAVEL ROAD |

La Moine • *Secondary Access (Delta)*
MI 4.1

Dog Creek • • *Dog Creek /Delta*
MI 3.6

To Redding *Lakeshore*
MI 0.0

1   0   1   2   3   4   5
MILES

his tippet, fishing one of his dark nymphs on the end and a dry on the dropper. The dry fly acted as an indicator for his nymph as well as catching its share of fish.

Fay died in 1983 and was eulogized by every outdoor writer who knew him. One of them said, "Fay never courted the publicity he received. He just came to regard it as a matter of fact. Although Fay preferred to fly fish, he never denigrated the way others like to fish—so long as it was moral and legal."

Since Fay's death his flies have become icons, proudly displayed in shadow boxes by their owners. Those who knew Fay realize that he would find this reverence amusing. He never took himself as seriously as those around him did. He was just a fisherman, and that's all that his flies were for.

Fay is gone, but Fred Gordon, a guide living in Dunsmuir, knows the Sacramento as well as anyone fishing it today.

Gordon's philosophy of fishing follows that of Fay: "Keep a close line and keep fishing."

According to Gordon, "Most anglers get hung up by a pretty piece of water. If you find fish, stay put. If not, move out." Gordon follows this philosophy—just try to keep up with him on a stream that is sparsely populated with fish. He makes a couple of casts to a spot, then to another, then another, then he moves up the river and works another small area.

He doesn't wait for fish to turn on in an area. They're given just a couple of chances at a fly. "The river has plenty of fish that are willing to hit, don't bother waiting for the others," he says. "Fish on up or down the river, and come back later."

Castle Crags, a State Park, is in the background. Frank Raymond

Patterns and Seasons: "Opening day is always good for me. I fish heavily weighted #6 Stonefly Nymphs because the river is usually high," says Gordon. "You have to get the nymph down to the fish, the water is cold and they aren't moving around."

Use a floating line with an indicator at the union of the fly line and the leader. A 3X or 4X leader is best because visibility isn't a problem and heavy line is needed to bring a heavy fish in against the strong current.

The period around opening day is usually fine for the upper Sacramento. But when the weather warms, runoff from the mountains raises the river too high for good fishing. If this happens at the beginning of the season, you may have to wait two or three weeks for the river to become fishable. A warm spell can bring melting snow, causing even colder water, which in turn makes the trout sluggish.

Angling strategies should consider the shape of the stream. Heavy runoff in the narrow upper river canyon above Cantara can raise the river a foot and a half, but in the lower canyon above the lake the river spreads out over gravel bars and may rise only an inch or so.

Hatches begin in the lower river and move up as the weather warms. The upper Sacramento doesn't have a significant morning fishery —most of the action begins to occur about three in the afternoon. Many anglers tend to start too early and burn out before the fishing turns on. Gordon prefers to fish the early morning with nymphs in the pocket water around Dunsmuir, then quit for lunch. He goes back out in the late afternoon, again fishing nymphs until he switches to dries in the evening and stays until dark.

As spring moves into summer, switch to lighter leaders and smaller flies—4X leader and #12 or #14 nymphs; AP Black, Hare's Ear, Hare's Tail, or PT Nymphs. Changing weather conditions mean you can never predict when you will have a daytime hatch. Gordon is always ready with a #14 Elk Hair Caddis or Cahill.

Gordon's number one fly is the Elk Hair Caddis because it imitates caddis, small stoneflies and mayflies. The current favorites on the river are the paraduns and parachutes.

A study documented 14 types of mayflies, 20 stoneflies and various caddis on the upper Sacramento. Through June, stones, caddis and mayflies are hatching. The fish in the Sacramento are opportunistic about nymphs, taking anything that comes along, but they may key in on a single dry fly pattern.

Gordon fishes baetis imitations in the mornings and blue wing olive imitations in the late evenings.

As the heat of summer increases, the good fishing continues to push back into evening. By July the river is fairly slow for anglers except from Mossbrae Falls through Dunsmuir. Mossbrae Falls is a series of lava springs that put 40-degree water into the river. The cold water allows hatches to continue into summer.

The upper river, from Dunsmuir to Sims, has good nymphing water—fast water broken by boulders and pockets. You can continuously wade and fish nymphs on the upper river because it is full of fish-holding pockets.

The lower river, from Sims to Shasta Lake, has long, deep areas where you must climb out of the stream, walk along the bank, then re-enter the stream through heavy brush.

The upper Sacramento is nearly completely accessible to the public. From Box Canyon Dam to the headwaters of Lake Shasta, Interstate 5 follows the stream, as does the Southern Pacific tracks. Freeway exits from I-5 are treated as primary access points for the purposes of this book. Once off the freeway almost all roads either end at or cross the tracks, which follow the river. Although the exits are spaced several miles apart, the angler who is willing to walk a few minutes will find that there is no part of the river that can't be reached.

Anglers with a second car can drop one off at one access and begin fishing from another.

The accesses will be described from the lowermost at Lakeshore going upriver to Ney Springs. The freeway mileage along Interstate 5 begins with "0.0" at Lakeshore. Miles will be the distance north of the Lakeshore Exit, which is 28 miles north of Redding. The primary exits are those with a freeway off ramp or major exit.

The secondary exits are roads that can be reached from the freeway but are not marked. Most of these are unimproved roads used by Southern Pacific for track maintenance. Most of these have gates that are not locked, but keep in mind that SP could change its mind about locking the gates at any time, particularly if vandalism or littering becomes a problem.

In 1985 two campers left a campfire unattended near Delta. The result was about 1,200 burned acres of timber

Cantara Loop offers excellent pocket water fishing. Brad Jackson

and brush. It goes without saying that these areas are scrutinized for campfires today and citations are issued without hesitation.

If you decide to camp along the Sacramento, please do it in one of the Forest Service or private campgrounds in the area.

Access

Lakeshore—Mile 0.0

This is the first river access above Shasta Lake. Take the Lakeshore Exit at Lakehead and turn right. Turn left at the T and follow Lakeshore 1.5 miles to the end of the pavement. A rough dirt road passes to the right of two houses and goes another 0.3 mile to the river. The road ends 0.6 mile from the end of the pavement. The river here has long, slow, deep pools with long tail-outs. This is a good bait and lure area. It is best fly fished early in the season when the hatches are prolific, or late when rainbows and browns from Shasta Lake come into the river to escape warm water.

Dog Creek—Mile 3.6

Heading north on I-5, this is a left side exit. Take the first left turn to Fenders Ferry Road and follow it 1 mile to a bridge spanning the river. A deep hole just below the bridge is popular for swimmers. Before the wild trout designation, this area was planted by the California Department of Fish and Game. The river can be accessed up or down stream by walking the tracks. It can be fished from the other side by walking up the sand and gravel bar that follows the river. A long riffle runs for a quarter mile above Dog Creek.

Delta—Mile 3.6

On the right side of I-5, directly across from the Dog Creek Exit, is the Delta Exit. Follow the first fork to the right 0.5 mile past a cluster of homes to a wide area next to the railroad tracks above the river. Park next to the fence that parallels the tracks and follow the trail that goes through a metal gate and down to the river. This area has long, fast pools with long riffles. Work nymphs through the pocket water during the day and during the hatches. Come back in the late evening with dries.

From the Sims Flat area of the river. A USFS camp ground is located here. Frank Raymond

Secondary Access—Mile 4.1

Approximately 0.5 mile past the Delta-Dog Creek Exit, on the right hand side of I-5, a metal gate at the edge of a pull-out off the freeway marks the beginning of a road that leads to the river. Go through the gate and follow the pavement for 0.6 mile. Pass the first dirt road to the right; continue on 100 yards further and turn right onto a second dirt road. Follow this road 0.6 mile to a flat area near a sharp bend in the river. Or you may continue to follow the road upriver along the tracks.

This area has long, slow pools and a couple of nice riffles. The riffle coming into the river bend can be fished from the opposite bank—wade the river at the end of the pool above the bend. An old rock retaining wall in the river is good for bait and lure fishermen and for dry flies at dusk. The tail-out is good for evening dries. By crossing the river you can fish upstream along the opposite bank for a short ways before it becomes steep bluffs.

This area can also be accessed from La Moine by walking down the tracks.

La Moine—Mile 6.5

This is a left hand exit heading north. After the exit take the first road to the left, then stay to the right for 0.3 mile to the end of the road under the I-5 bridge. A 4X4 road takes you a short way to the end of the road next to the tracks. A staircase of riffles can be fished from the other side of the river. Wading here would be tough. By staying on a dirt road on the left side of Slate Creek you can follow the river a short distance upstream to a series of long riffles.

Below La Moine the river flattens out into a chain of long pools all the way to Shasta Lake. Lots of trout are taken in this area because they come out of the lake to spawn or to avoid warm water in the lake, especially late in the season.

Be selective in this lower area—don't expect fish to be everywhere as on the upper river. Fish the riffles with nymphs and watch the pools for rising fish. Walk around the pool to the next riffle. If you don't see fish rising, move on and come back later. If you see only one or two risers move to the next pool and observe it for a short while. Don't sit on a pool waiting for it to come on; if it isn't happening, move on.

Pollard Flat—Mile 7.9

Pollard Flat does not have a direct access to the river. To get to this area take the secondary exit 0.6 mile north.

Secondary Access—Mile 8.5

This is the first road north of Pollard Flat. Turn right past a chain link fence, through a gate, and follow the road a short distance to the river. From there you can take the left fork upriver a short ways or cross the tracks and continue on to a bridge with a locked gate.

This is a tough area to fish because the long, slow pools are lined with brush and trees. The river flattens out and gradually slows as it approaches Shasta Lake. This is not considered the best section of river although it certainly is one of the prettiest.

Gibson—Mile 10.1

This exit has been closed for construction of a new freeway bridge but it will reopen. Follow it to the right one mile to where it ends near the railroad tracks. Park, and walk up or down the river. A few good riffles are downriver with long pools in between. A walk upriver will bring you to deep pools and narrow slots, with some riffles. This is a popular bait fishing area.

Secondary Access/Shiloah—Mile 11.9

A road to the right crosses the crest of a ridge then drops a short ways toward the river. Cars can park at the top, trucks can drive the short distance to the end of the road. Follow a trail down to the tracks. Across the river is a beautiful sandy beach and a very deep pool. This is a favorite stopping place for rafters during the early spring runoff. You can walk upriver along the tracks and fish a series of rapids, or pocket water and riffles above the rapid. Walk downriver to a series of riffles and pools.

Secondary Access/Shotgun Creek—Mile 12.4

A steep, paved road drops off the right hand side of I-5 from a wide pull-out. The road is okay for cars. Park here and walk, or follow the road upriver paralleling the tracks to Shotgun Creek, which marks the upper boundary of the Wild Trout Section of the river. This is the easiest way to access the area from Shotgun Creek down.

Shotgun Creek (Left side exit)—Mile 12.7

The Wild Trout Section that runs from Shotgun Creek to Lake Shasta begins here. There are no restrictions on bait or tackle, but the limit is two fish per person. Some pocket water exists below Shotgun Creek but pools predominate. By working your way upriver you may catch planted and holdover planted fish that were put into the river at Sims.

Note: This area of the river is easier to access from the secondary access either to the north before the Sims Exit, or from the secondary access to the south.

Immediately to the right a dirt road leads through an open gate to Shotgun Creek and a flat parking area. Park here and walk through the culvert that runs under I-5. At the other end climb out on the left side of the creek and follow a trail that bends to the right. The trail crosses an old highway, then continues on to the railroad tracks. Cross a trestle over the creek, then follow the trail down the right hand side of Shotgun Creek to the river.

There is an excellent riffle right at the mouth of Shotgun Creek. The best fishing is upstream toward Sims Campground where you may encounter holdover fish that were planted at Sims.

Secondary Access—Mile 13.5

At the north end of a large cut, just before a guardrail, a road turns off to the right between several large boulders. Follow the road 0.4 mile to the bottom of the hill and park at the end of the road.

Shotgun Creek comes in just downriver. This area has good pools and riffles and is the easiest access to the area above Shotgun Creek.

Walking the railroad tracks provides access to secluded fishing. Brad Jackson

Sims Road—Mile 14.2

Follow the paved road to the bottom of the hill or cross the bridge to the Sims campground. The best access is along the rail road tracks on the west side of the river. A paved road to the left ends along the tracks after 0.2 mile.

This area has riffles and fast-flowing holes with pocket water and side slots. Overhanging brush and elephant ears are in abundance. This is the lowest area where trout are planted in the river. This area is popular with bait and lure anglers, especially from the Sims Campground side.

Mossbrae Falls. Dale Lackey

Secondary Access—Mile 16.1

A road to the right leads down the hill to the tracks. This area has excellent riffles which are good for nymphs and dries, half pocket water, half pools. At Sims the pools get longer and slower.

Flume Creek—Mile 16.3

Park at the off ramp and follow the trail through blackberry bushes down the hill and across the tracks to the river. This area is easier to access from the secondary access to the south.

Conant—Mile 17.4

At Conant the river slows even more, creating pools. From Conant downriver to Flume Creek there is little change. The pools are a little deeper but the river still has a good flow of current. At the Conant Exit a road leads off to the right then forks. Take either fork, park at the end of the road and walk to the river. The tracks allow access anywhere along this side of the river. The river in this area is primarily fast riffles and pools, good for dry flies.

Sweetbriar—Mile 18.6

Turn left, go 0.3 mile to the end of the road and park next to the tracks. Turn right, proceed 0.5 mile to where the road crosses the tracks. A sign welcomes anglers to park near the tracks and to walk in. This is a good idea since the one-lane bridge crosses the river into a summer home area where parking is non-existent. The river flows through banks reinforced with concrete, channelizing it and making it too deep for good wading.

Considering the ease of access to other areas, fishing here doesn't make a lot of sense.

Castella—Mile 20.4

Take the Castella Exit. Since the road to the right leads to an area where private homes block access to the river, go left and drive 0.5 mile to a bridge that crosses the river. Turn left toward the Castle Crags picnic area, where the river can be entered. This is mostly pocket water with a sprinkling of pools. This is more diverse than the water through Dunsmuir. Castle Creek, which is not good fishing, enters the Sacramento here.

Soda Creek—Mile 22.1

Turn right after the exit and follow the paved road 0.3 mile to the river and park on either side of the bridge. Work up or down the river along the tracks or through the brush. A large, deep pool under the bridge is a favorite with bait and lure anglers, and swimmers.

DUNSMUIR

The area through Dunsmuir is excellent nymphing water with nearly unlimited access. You can fish almost the entire stream just by wading the river, which averages about a foot-and-a-half deep and is loaded with boulders and pockets.

Here are the accesses to the Sacramento in Dunsmuir. Mileage is included when they are exits from I-5:

Railroad Park: From the sewage plant below the Railroad Park bridge to the Soda Creek Bridge is a little over a mile. This is an awkward stretch of the river full of pea gravel and few holding spots.

Crag View Drive/Railroad Park: Mile 23.7: Take the South First Street exit. After the exit, turn left, follow the road past a mobile home park, then turn right onto South First Avenue. Follow South First to a bridge that crosses the river. Park on the west side of the bridge. The stream can be entered from the bridge. South First follows the river upstream and can be used for access anywhere that you can park your car. Do not park in driveways or yards.

Butterfly Bridge: Follow South First Street upriver to its intersection with Butterfly Avenue, turn left to the bridge. The river can be accessed at the bridge and along Butterfly Avenue.

Sacramento Bridge: Continue upstream along South First then follow a jog onto Sacramento Avenue. Follow the river upstream to the Sacramento Bridge. Access is plentiful here.

I-5 Bridge: Follow Sacramento Avenue upstream until it passes under the I-5 Freeway bridge. This whole area is accessible. The railroad tracks across the river can be walked for unlimited river access. Follow Stagecoach Avenue all the way out to the intersection with Dunsmuir Avenue.

Dunsmuir City Park: The drive to Dunsmuir City Park passes between the softball park and an old steam locomotive on display. The park has very good fishing considering the amount of pressure it receives.

Shasta Retreat or Scarlett Way: This is the last Dunsmuir access. Follow Dunsmuir Avenue north to a metal arch that says "Shasta Retreat/Scarlett Way." This area is heavily planted and fished by lure and bait anglers, but a short hike upstream takes you into an incredible native trout fishery. A few houses come right down to the water across the river, but they don't seem to affect the fishing. Begin fishing once you pass an old footbridge that has been washed out. Shasta Retreat upstream to Mossbrae Falls is considered by many to be the best stretch of water on the river.

Mount Shasta

Cantara to Shasta Retreat: This stretch of water takes you past Mossbrae Falls. It is approximately 3 miles long with plenty of water for a good day's fishing. Mossbrae Falls is easy to recognize since water cascades right out of the side of the canyon. Mossbrae is a mile and a half upriver from Shasta Retreat Bridge.

Cantara Loop—Mile 32.0

Take the McCloud/Mt. Shasta Exit, then take the first right onto Azalea. Turn right and follow the road across I-5 and keep going until you cross the railroad tracks. Turn left and proceed 0.4 mile to Cantara Street, turn right. Follow Cantara 1.3 miles to the bottom of the hill and on to the river. Park where the road meets the river.

Ney Springs—Mile 32.0

This is the uppermost access to the Sacramento River. Take the first Mount Shasta Exit, immediately past the McCloud Exit, onto Mount Shasta Boulevard. Follow it to the Lamplighter Restaurant on the left and turn left onto Ream Avenue. Follow Ream to its intersection with W.A. Barr Road and turn left. Follow W.A. Barr Road about two miles, cross Box Canyon Dam and turn left onto Castle Lake Road. About 100 yards up Castle Lake Road, take the first left onto a dirt road. Follow it to the Ney Springs Fishing Access, follow that to the end of the road. Follow the trail to the river.

For More Information:

Fred Gordon, 6283 Gillis St., Dunsmuir, CA 96025, (916) 235-2673 • Joe Kimsey, Ted Fay Fly Shop, 44310 Dunsmuir Ave., Dunsmuir, CA 96025, (916) 235-2969 • The Fly Shop, 4140 Churn Creek Rd., Redding, CA 96002, (916) 222-3555.

Dog Creek Bridge. Dale Lackey

Chapter Four

LOWER SACRAMENTO RIVER

The Lower Sacramento, from Keswick Dam to Red Bluff, is the most underrated trophy trout stream in California.

The prime area for trout is from the Rodeo Grounds in Redding downstream to Balls Ferry. Fishing this area requires a boat—there is little public access and it is too wide and too swift to fish adequately from shore. Public launch ramps are located at the Posse Grounds in Redding, at Anderson River Park and at Balls Ferry near Cottonwood.

The flow into the lower Sacramento from Shasta Dam is controlled by the Bureau of Reclamation. The water entering the lake from the upper Sacramento River, Pit River, McCloud River and Squaw Creek is stored in Shasta Lake, then released down the lower Sacramento as it is needed. Much of it is earmarked for irrigation in the Central Valley, to hold back salt water intrusion into the Delta and for municipal water districts. Releases for fish environment or for recreation are low priority.

Through the winter, the flows are cut to a minimum of 2,600 cubic feet per second (c.f.s.) to allow Shasta Lake to fill. As the lake nears full, releases are increased to maintain a cushion for flood control.

As the weather warms, Central Valley agriculture demands escalate and the flows are increased to 7,000 or 8,000 c.f.s through April and into May. During the peak demand months of late spring and summer they increase to a maximum of 14,000 c.f.s.

The best trout fishing occurs in late winter and early spring when the flows are at a minimum. The fish in the river are concentrated and the current is at its most fishable. This is also the time of year when aquatic insects begin hatching. Caddis in its various stages are the primary food source of the trophy rainbows in this stretch of the river.

Brad Jackson

TECHNIQUE

Bait: Bait anglers have the best success on night crawlers or crickets, although some do use salmon eggs and Power Bait. The angler runs the boat to the upper end of the pool, casts upstream and lets the boat drift through the pool, dragging the bait along the bottom. Another method is to keep the boat next to a holding area and drift fish the bait through the area.

During the salmon spawn, Glo Bugs also produce when fished this way.

Lures: Back trolling Hot Shots, Wee Warts or other diving plugs from drift boats is growing in popularity on this part of the river. Using a technique developed for steelhead fishing on coastal streams, the oarsman holds the boat against the current while the angler runs a Hot Shot 30 to 50 feet downstream from the boat. The Hot Shot has a blade at its head that pulls the lure under the surface and makes it vibrate in the current.

The plug is worked slowly through the pool. When it enters a fish's territory it is regarded as an intruder or a smaller food fish and attacked. Regardless of how the trout views the plug the result is the same.

In late winter when the flows are at their lowest, spinners can be a key producer. Terry Hopper, a Central Valley sportsman, likes to cast Panther Martin spinners upstream, then keep a tight line as the lure drifts back in the current. "You don't have to retrieve furiously," says Hopper. "Just let the blades work in the current."

Fly Fishing: Fly fishing centers on the caddis, the prominent insect in the lower Sacramento. In spring bushes along the river are loaded with adult caddis and hatches become so prolific that the air is filled with clouds of swarming insects. During the spinner fall, dead caddis can actually mat the river surface.

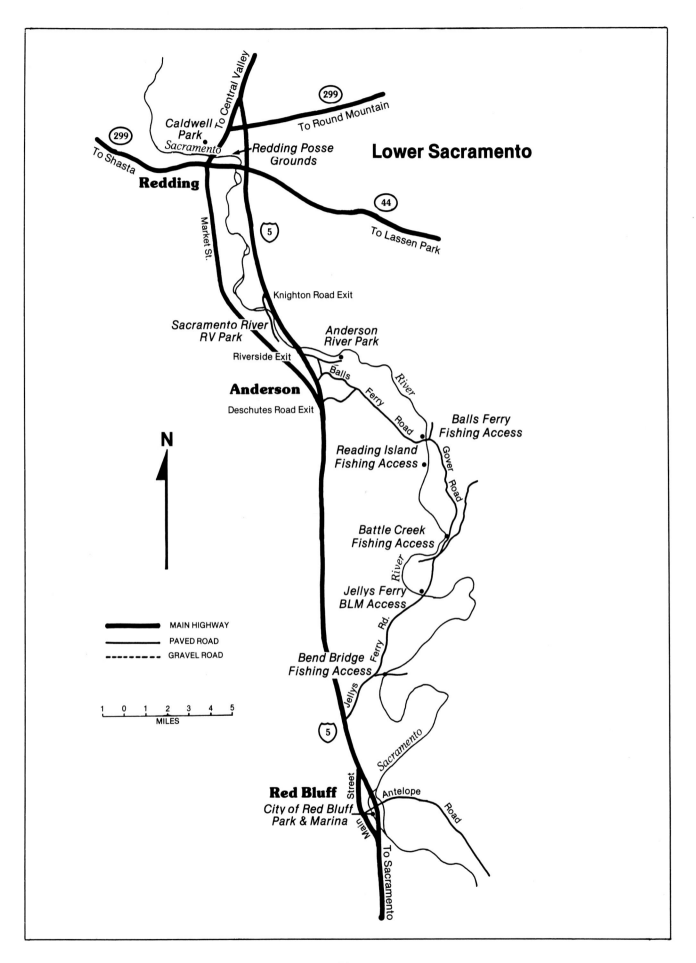

Lower Sacramento

299

To Central Valley

299 To Round Mountain

Caldwell Park
Sacramento
Redding Posse Grounds

299 To Shasta

Redding

44 To Lassen Park

5

Market St.

Knighton Road Exit

Sacramento River RV Park

Anderson River Park

Riverside Exit

Balls Ferry Road

River

Anderson

Deschutes Road Exit

Balls Ferry Fishing Access

Reading Island Fishing Access

Gover Road

N

Battle Creek Fishing Access

River

Jellys Ferry BLM Access

MAIN HIGHWAY
PAVED ROAD
GRAVEL ROAD

Jellys Ferry Rd.

Bend Bridge Fishing Access

1 0 1 2 3 4 5
MILES

Jellys

5

Sacramento

Red Bluff

Main Street

Antelope

City of Red Bluff Park & Marina

Road

To Sacramento

23

Muscular and robust, 'Lower Sac' 'bows have earned a reputation as supercharged gamefish. The river's fast and fertile current get principal credit for its rainbows fighting qualities. Brad Jackson

George Durand, one of the few guides who takes fly anglers on the lower Sacramento, feels so confident in caddis that he seldom fishes with anything else, even though all four types of aquatic insects are represented.

A distant second is the midge hatch. Durand says that at times rainbows to 10 pounds have been caught on midge pupa imitations. Mayflies are active during the summer months. Durand says to watch for baetis mayflies on overcast days since they prefer the subdued light of a cloudy day. Stoneflies are represented by Little Sallys (little yellow stones) and large salmon flies.

He advises anglers fishing the stream in early spring or late summer to be armed with imitations of October caddis. Durand floats the stream watching for rising fish. He pulls the boat in and wades out above the rising fish, or casts from the anchored boat, and uses a downstream presentation to dead drift the fly to the trout.

During mid-day, Durand fishes #12 and #14 Caddis Pupas, LaFontaine Pupas, Zug Bugs or Birds Nests. Fishing the pupa under an indicator and with a sink tip line, watch for swirling fish and cast so the pupa swings right in front of them.

In the evenings when the fish rise for adult caddis, Durand switches to Elk Hair Caddis.

The midge hatch can occur at any time of year, particularly in the summer evenings.

During the little yellow stone hatch, Durand fishes a light-bodied Hare's Ear Nymph. Salmon flies can happen at any time early to late spring.

In late summer and early fall, watch for October caddis.

"October caddis don't seem to follow traditional patterns on the lower Sacramento," says Durand. "They might come off in late spring and again in fall."

Durand considers the spring months the best time to be on the river. When the flows reach 8,000 or 9,000 c.f.s. and the daily temperatures exceed the century mark, fly fishing becomes tough, although Durand notes that "a lot of guys like fishing Glo Bugs in the summer when salmon are spawning."

Glo Bugs also can be fished with spinning gear during the high flows of summer. Use enough pencil lead or split shot to get the Glo Bug down to the bottom, which is next to impossible to do by fly fishing.

Access Boat Launch Ramps

The most effective way to fish the lower Sacramento River is by boat. Although the river is the largest in California, its fast, free-flowing character creates shallow tail-outs and rapids.

The long, fast-flowing pools with shallow riffles make jet boats the most suitable craft.

Propeller-powered boats may be able to maneuver along the river during the summer when flows are high, but it's always a matter of time before someone finds a rock in mid-riffle that sticks up a little higher than the operator thought. And the Sacramento is no place to be without power.

Drift boats, the type used in the Northwest for steelhead fishing, are becoming popular because they can float over shallow areas and are very maneuverable. The only drawback is that they can only go downriver. A vehicle must be left at a downriver takeout location or the anglers may find themselves faced with a long walk back to their starting point.

Public launch ramps are at the following locations:

Caldwell Park in Redding

This is located at Lake Redding Park, where North Market Street crosses the Sacramento River. This area requires motor boats that can go upstream because the Anderson Cottonwood Irrigation District dam is located a few hundred yards down from the launch ramp.

Redding Posse Grounds

Take Highway 299 West from Interstate 5, take the Park Marina off-ramp. Turn right onto Auditorium Way, follow the road to the right and drive past the Redding Civic Auditorium to a parking lot near the horse stables. The launch ramp is at the upriver end of the parking lot.

This ramp is located on one of the best pools in the river. Anglers drift bait or back troll plugs down either side of the river, or sweep the tail-out located in mid-river near some old pilings.

Any of the riffles and pools in this area have large populations of rainbows. This is also the most heavily-fished trout water on the lower Sacramento.

There are more excellent riffles in the eight miles between Redding and Anderson than a good angler can fish in a day. Most of the water is good riffle water for fly fishing or pools for back trolling.

Sacramento River RV Park, (916) 365-6402, 8900 Riverland Drive, Redding, CA 96002.

This is a private launch facility where a fee is charged and access could be denied at any time.

Eight miles south of Redding on Interstate 5, take the Knighton Road Exit toward the river and turn left onto Riverland Drive. Two miles later, at the end of the road, you will pass through a white arch marking the boundary of the Sacramento River RV Park. Stop at the office to register and pay a day-use fee. If no one is in the office, you can self-register. Follow the road as it winds to the left, across a dry wash, and on to the paved launch ramp and dock area.

Anderson River Park

Take the Riverside Exit from I-5 and turn east. When Riverside dead ends into North Street, turn right. Take the second left onto Willow Street, then follow Willow to where a small blue sign at the corner of Willow and Rupert marks the entrance to Anderson River Park.

This area has a paved launch ramp, parking and restrooms.

Balls Ferry Fishing Access

Take the Balls Ferry Exit into Anderson, turn east. Follow Balls Ferry Road to the intersection with Deschutes Road. Turn left 200 yards, turn right at McGee's Corner as Balls Ferry Road continues to wind eastward. Where a sign indicates Ash Creek Road and Balls Ferry Resort to the left, turn left onto Ash Creek Road. Continue to the bridge over the Sacramento—the launch ramp is immediately to the right, Rooster's Landing is to the left.

Reading Island

This access has not been well maintained and motor boats may have a tough time maneuvering through the slough to get to the main river.

Take the Balls Ferry Exit into Anderson and turn east. Follow Balls Ferry Road to the intersection with Deschutes Road. Turn left 200 yards, then turn right at McGee's Corner as Balls Ferry Road continues to wind eastward past Ash Creek Road. Continue on Balls Ferry Road to Reading Island Fishing Access.

The Lower Sacramento is big water; you must carve the intimidating flows into readable components. Deeply-fished caddis larva and pupa are particularly effective. Brad Jackson

Battle Creek Fishing Access
Unimproved gravel bar launching

Take the Balls Ferry Exit into Anderson, turn east. Follow Balls Ferry Road to the intersection with Deschutes Road. Turn left 200 yards, turn right at McGee's Corner as Balls Ferry Road continues to wind eastward. A sign indicates Ash Creek Road and Balls Ferry Resort to the left, turn left onto Ash Creek Road. Continue to the bridge over the Sacramento. The launch ramp is immediately to the right, Rooster's Landing is to the left.

Turn right onto Gover Road and continue for several miles. The road makes a dog-leg to the right toward the river then left again and becomes Jellys Ferry Road. A gravel road turns off into blackberry bushes and leads to a gravel bar on the river. Boats can be launched off the gravel bar by four-wheel drive trucks.

Bend Bridge Public Fishing Access
Paved launch

Take the Jellys Ferry Exit from I-5, turn east. Follow Jellys Ferry Road to the Bend Store, cross the bridge and turn right to the launch ramp and parking area.

The Sacramento as it runs through town. Frank Raymond

City of Red Bluff Park and Marina
Paved launch ramp and parking area

Take the Central Red Bluff Exit and cross the river to the light on Main Street. Turn left two blocks, then turn left onto Marina Drive to reach the launch ramp and parking area.

Walk-in Access

The lower Sacramento has very few places where an angler can walk to the river without crossing private property. An attempt is under way to acquire riparian areas to be used for public access, but that is a long way off.

Caldwell Park
Redding

Located where North Market Street crosses the Sacramento River, the north side of the river is a city park that borders the river. This area hasn't been explored enough to comment on the quality of the fishing.

The Sacramento River Trail on the south side follows the river seven miles upstream to Keswick Dam, making the full length of the river accessible. The river is generally fast-flowing through this area.

The Posse Grounds and Turtle Bay

Right in the heart of downtown Redding is one of the most overlooked fishing areas in California.

Take Highway 299 West from Interstate 5, then take the Park Marina off-ramp. Turn right onto Auditorium Way, follow the road to the right and drive past the Redding Civic Auditorium.

The angler can walk into any part of the river in this area. A parking area near a concrete amphitheater marks a good riffle that anglers can wade. Fishing is good in the tail-out above the riffle as well as below it.

By walking in near the concrete monolith, the angler will find a huge area of gravel. The gravel for Shasta Dam was hauled by train from this area up the river to the dam site. It is one of the most consistent areas to fish with bait or lures for trout.

East Turtle Bay Regional Park

Take the Cypress Exit from I-5 and turn west. At the first light, turn right onto Bechelli Lane. Follow Bechelli about two miles past the offices and homes to where it turns and drops sharply off the hill to a flat area near the river. This is just across the river from the park described in the preceding section.

Fish this area with crawlers, eggs, Glo Bugs, spinners, or back trolled Hot Shots.

Anderson River Park

The next area an angler can reach by foot without crossing private property is at Anderson River Park. Take the Riverside Exit from I-5 and turn east. Turn right onto North Lane, then left onto Willow. About 5 blocks farther, at Rupert Avenue, a small blue sign on the left indicates Anderson River Park.

Battle Creek

Take the Balls Ferry Exit into Anderson, turn east. Follow Balls Ferry Road to the intersection with Deschutes Road. Turn left 200 yards, then right at McGee's Corner as Balls Ferry Road continues to wind eastward. A sign indicates Ash Creek Road and Balls Ferry Resort to the left, turn left onto Ash Creek Road. Continue to the bridge over the Sacramento at Balls Ferry. The launch ramp is immediately to the right; Rooster's Landing is to the left.

Turn right onto Parkville Road and continue for several miles. The road makes a dog-leg to the right toward the river then left again and becomes Jellys Ferry Road. A gravel road turns off into blackberry bushes and leads to a gravel bar on the river.

Slightly upstream of Battle Creek is the Barge Hole, famous for the numbers of salmon that hold there waiting to enter Battle Creek and the Coleman Fish Hatchery.

For More Information:

George Durand, 1065 De Moll Dr., Redding CA 96002, (916) 222-5630. Fly Shop Outfitters, 4140 Churn Creek Road, Redding, CA 96002, (916) 222-3555. Hank Mautz, 3231 Davey Way, Anderson, CA 96007, (916) 365-1447. Tom Stanton, Fish Tales Guide Service, P.O. Box 1411, Hayfork, CA 96041, (916) 628-5176.

Sunset hatches and ovipositing flights of caddis sponsor stimulating dry fly fishing for rainbows that frequently exceed 20 inches. Brad Jackson

Chapter Five

LAKE SISKIYOU AND LAKE SHASTA

LAKE SISKIYOU

The first time I fished the Sacramento was during college in the early 1960s. A friend and I took the road out of Mount Shasta and across the Steel Bridge at the entrance to Box Canyon. We followed the road upriver and began fishing. The weather turned nasty, it started raining and eventually turned to snow. My friend's car wouldn't start and we ended up walking back to town.

I caught one fish that day, a six-inch rainbow. Hardly an auspicious beginning for such a great stream.

The road we used, as well as the part of the stream we fished, is now under the water of Lake Siskiyou. Formed behind the Box Canyon Dam built in the 1960s, it is open to the public as a fine trout fishing lake. During the winter and spring of 1972 I used to drive from my home in McCloud to fish the north shore with night crawlers. Catching a limit of five 12-inch rainbows was easy in those days.

Like a lot of lakes, Siskiyou's fishing has since deteriorated. It still boasts good fishing, but the lake is popular as a vacation area and summer visitors seem to catch the fish as fast as they are planted.

The lake is slowly gaining a reputation as a smallmouth bass lake, but I doubt that it will ever achieve the reputation enjoyed by Lake Shasta, Trinity Lake, or even nearby Lake Shastina. I've seen smallmouth that I know would top five pounds.

The best area for bank anglers to fish is along the north shore. Take W.A. Barr Road out of Mount Shasta and turn right onto North Shore Road. Follow it across Wagon Creek and along the lake where the road winds through the trees. Several undeveloped parking areas can be seen from the road. Park in any of them, bait up with a crawler, Power Bait or Pautzke Fireball, cast the line out, and let it soak.

Frank Raymond

If trolling, a very hot technique is to tie a dark fly onto the monofilament with either very little or no weight and troll slowly, dragging the fly in the surface film.

Trollers also use small Rapalas and any of the various spinners and spoons on the market.

LAKE SHASTA

Shasta Lake is the largest reservoir in California. Although it is considered one of the finest bass lakes in the West, it doesn't have a great reputation for trout.

Except for a small cadre of anglers, no one seems to take trout fishing seriously at Shasta Lake. People do not go to Shasta for the trout fishing, although they may hang a rod off the side of a houseboat once they get there.

Trout angling is best in the early to late spring, while the lake surface is cool. Trophy trout to seven and eight pounds are caught often this time of year.

During this period the trout feed near the surface on schools of threadfin shad, a tiny baitfish. As the lake surface warms, the trout are driven deeper to find cool water.

The trout fishing this time of year is unsophisticated as fishing techniques go. Most anglers use a bobber and a minnow. A Shur-Stop goes on the line first. This is a tiny piece of thin, flat metal a quarter-inch long with a hole in each end. The line goes through one hole, makes a wrap around the metal, then goes through the other hole. Its purpose is to allow the bobber to slide up or down the line to the length you want the bobber above the bait.

Tie on a barrel swivel to keep the bobber from sliding against the hook when casting. Hook the minnow behind the dorsal fin so it can swim around. A couple of split shot a foot or so above the hook will keep the minnow near the bottom. You can also use crayfish, crawlers, crickets or Power Bait.

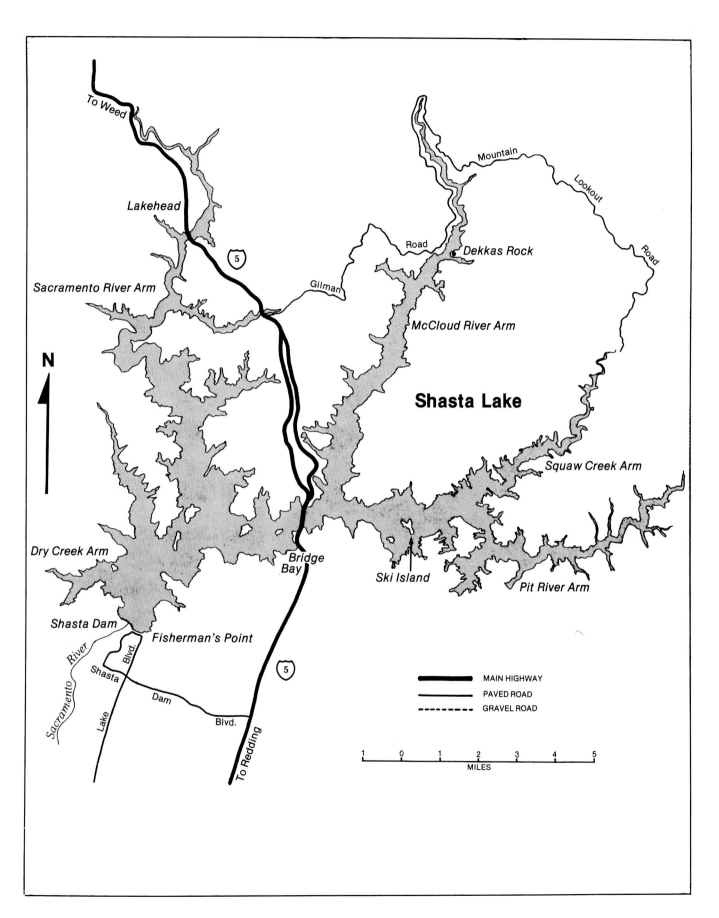

To Weed

Lakehead

5

Sacramento River Arm

Mountain

Lookout

Road

Road

Gilman

Dekkas Rock

McCloud River Arm

N

Shasta Lake

Squaw Creek Arm

Dry Creek Arm

Bridge
Bay

Ski Island

Pit River Arm

Shasta Dam

Fisherman's Point

Sacramento River

Blvd.

Shasta

Dam

Lake

Blvd.

5

To Redding

MAIN HIGHWAY

PAVED ROAD

GRAVEL ROAD

| 1 | 0 | 1 | 2 | 3 | 4 | 5 |

MILES

The easiest area to fish from shore is near the dam, from Fishermen's Point on the south side to the Dry Creek arm on the north shore.

As the lake surface warms and drives the fish deeper, trollers use downriggers to get Kastmasters and other shad imitations down to the fish, often to 80 feet or more.

Bank anglers can still fish with crawlers and minnows when fish are deep. Simply run the line down to the depth the fish are working. Much of the bank at Shasta Lake is very steep, so by casting out and letting the bait sink, anglers can get their bait down to almost any depth.

According to Darryl Moulton and Gracie Valentine at Bridge Bay Marina, the best fishing is in the main channel of the lake, from the lower reaches of the main arms to the dam.

Anglers fishing the Sacramento River arm will find the best fishing occurs from the O'Brien Creek Inlet downstream to the dam. Anglers on the McCloud arm have the most success from the Shasta Caverns to the mouth on the main body of the lake. From the caverns back into the arm to Dekkas Rock, fishing is spotty. The McCloud is con-

sidered to be the best trout fishing arm on the lake. From the mouth of Squaw Creek and the Pit River to the Mc-Cloud River arm is where the biggest fish in the lake are caught — trout that run from two to six pounds are caught near Ski Island.

"A lot of nice fish are caught right in Bridge Bay, too," says Moulton.

Trout aren't the only fish in the lake — Shasta is well-known for small, spotted and black bass. It also has a healthy catfish population along with bluegill and crappie. An angler who was fishing near Ski Island in July of 1989 even landed a 173-1/2 pound sturgeon.

Sturgeon have been landlocked in Shasta Lake since the dam was built in 1949. Anglers began fishing for them several years ago but success has been very limited. Moulton likes to tell the story of a time he went fishing and his rod began sliding into the water. He grabbed it but the 12-pound test line was running off the reel so fast he thought the drag was loose. By the time he tried to tighten the drag, the line came to the end and broke off. Then he tested the drag and found that it had been tightened down the whole time.

Here the lake is near to full, from the approach to the I-5 bridge. Frank Raymond

The Three Shastas—Shasta Dam, Shasta Lake and Mount Shasta. Frank Raymond

Access

Shasta Lake has 370 miles of shoreline, more than San Francisco Bay. To describe each fishing area would require a book in itself.

But any place where you can walk to the water line and throw a line in could be as good as any other.

Fishermen's Point

To reach the dam, take Shasta Dam Boulevard/Central Valley Exit from I-5 four miles north of Redding. Stay on Shasta Dam Boulevard to the Lake Boulevard intersection and turn right. When you reach the lake, turn left toward the dam. You will come to a parking area and a sign marking Fishermen's Point fishing access. Park in the lot and take the trail down to the lake shore.

You can fish wherever the trail meets the water's edge or work back toward the dam where the shoreline is heavily rip-rapped with large boulders.

Although it is a tough climb, many anglers prefer the rip-rap area because crawfish, a favorite food source for trout and bass, can hide in the rocks.

Dry Creek Arm

Follow the road across the dam and turn to the right onto a gravel road. Follow it to an unimproved parking area. Fish off any of the points in this area or hike up the lake to the Dry Creek arm.

Sacramento River Arm

Drive north of Redding on Interstate 5 to Lakehead.

You can turn onto Sugarloaf Road and fish down the Sacramento Arm or turn right to Antlers and the public launch ramp.

McCloud River Arm

Continue north on I-5 to Salt Creek Road and turn right. Follow the road 17 miles along the McCloud arm, cross the McCloud River bridge and drive to the campground. When the lake level is low, this area of the McCloud is a free-flowing stream. Before you get excited, it is nothing at all like the famed lower McCloud. Here, it is full of silt and is lifeless.

If the lake level is up, this area is stocked by the DFG. In the fall, rainbows and browns congregate in the arm waiting to enter the stream to spawn.

Squaw Creek Arm

Continue on past the McCloud Bridge campground to where the road dead ends to reach the Squaw Creek Arm. Little is known about fishing the lake in this area.

Pit River Arm

The upper Pit River Arm of Shasta Lake is virtually unreachable by vehicle.

For More Information:

Shasta Cascade Wonderland Association, 1250 Parkview, Redding, CA 96001, (916) 243-2643 • Phil Matsuida, Phil's Propellers, 3037 Twin View Blvd., Redding, CA 96003, (916) 275-4939.

Chapter Six

McCLOUD RIVER

The McCloud is the quintessential free-stone stream, a year-round flow of clear, cold water coursing through a wild, lush canyon. The wild strain of rainbows in the McCloud are gallant, hard-fighting fish. And the river's fast-flowing character gives them little time to consider whether the fly passing through the feeding zone is natural or a deception.

The McCloud is recognized as having one of the finest strains of wild trout in the world. In the late 19th Century eggs taken from the Shasta strain of rainbows in the McCloud River were used to stock streams in the eastern United States and ultimately streams throughout Europe.

Dale Lackey

The hatchery where those eggs were taken, which was located near O'Brien, now is covered by the waters of Shasta Lake.

In turn, brown trout from Europe were stocked in the McCloud. Although the McCloud is noted for its rainbow fishery, its brown trout population is a sleeping giant waiting to be discovered. The McCloud also was the southern-most habitat for Dolly Varden, but they apparently died out nearly two decades ago.

As the McCloud Dam tamed the flows of the lower river, it began to channelize, creating the long, slow pools that big browns thrive in. Each fall, browns migrate into the upper reaches of the lower McCloud to spawn. Huge browns to 10 pounds and more hold at the tail-outs until their eggs ripen. Then, with powerful thrusts of their tails they dig into the gravel and deposit their eggs before returning to the lake. As a result, fishing in the late fall is the best time to be on the river, but most anglers seem compelled to come during the worst time—opening weekend.

Access

The city of McCloud is nine miles east of Mount Shasta City. From Interstate 5 take the McCloud, Highway 89 Exit at the south end of Mount Shasta. From the exit to central McCloud at the Southern Avenue intersection is 9.4 miles. To reach the upper McCloud River continue east on Highway 89; to reach the Lower McCloud, turn right at the Shell station onto Southern Avenue. Southern Avenue becomes Squaw Valley Road as it leaves McCloud and continues south.

The intersection of Highway 89 and Southern Avenue is the point of origin—0.0 miles—for this chapter on the McCloud River.

McCloud River Loop Road

The McCloud River Loop Road, 6.2 miles from McCloud on Highway 89, was acquired by the U.S. Forest Service in 1989 from Champion Timberlands in a land trade. It parallels the McCloud for 5.4 miles, largely within shouting distance of the river. The road begins near Fowler's Campground and ends at Cattle Camp, the only developed campgrounds on the loop.

The easy access provided to the area by the road has resulted in heavy use. It is a popular camping, picnicking and fishing area. The unimproved road becomes powdery dust by mid-summer and the stream receives almost relentless fishing pressure.

The Loop Road is marked by the U.S. Forest Service sign for the Fowler's Campground where you will turn right. One-half mile from the turnoff the road intersects a logging road designated USFS 40N44.

Fowler's Campground

To reach Fowler's Campground go straight ahead. After a short distance the road forks. The left fork leads to Fowler's Campground, the right fork goes to Lower Falls, then continues a short distance along the the river before it

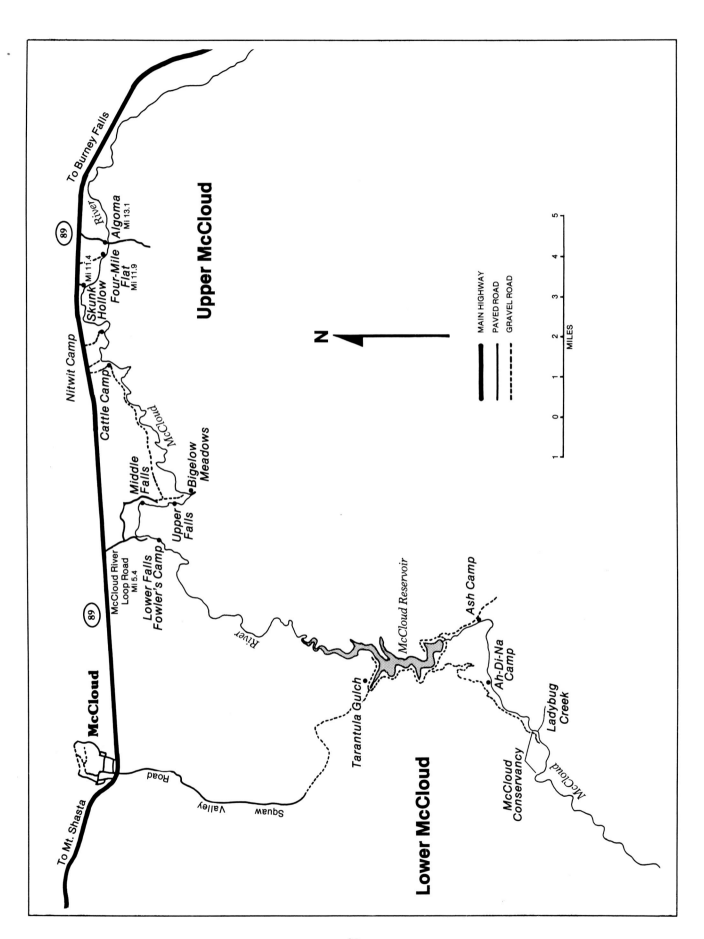

To Burney Falls

89

River

Algoma
Mi 13.1

Skunk Mi 11.4
Hollow
Four-Mile
Flat
Mi 11.9

Upper McCloud

Nitwit Camp

Cattle Camp

Middle
Falls

McCloud

Bigelow
Meadows

Upper
Falls

McCloud River
Loop Road
Mi 5.4

Lower Falls
Fowler's Camp

River

89

McCloud

To Mt. Shasta

Squaw

Valley Road

Road

Tarantula Gulch

McCloud Reservoir

Ash Camp

Ah-Di-Na
Camp

Lower McCloud

McCloud
Conservancy

Ladybug
Creek

McCloud

N

MAIN HIGHWAY
PAVED ROAD
GRAVEL ROAD

1   0   1   2   3   4   5
MILES

dead-ends. This is the lowest part of the river accessible to the public above McCloud Reservoir.

Below Fowler's campground the river enters the private property of the Hearst family.

This is also the most heavily fished area on the river and the campground is normally full throughout summer.

This part of the river is in a narrow, lava gorge surrounded by tall conifers. A canopy of willow and alder throws shade on the river most of the day. Elephant ear, fern, and bunch grass are found throughout the river.

Middle Falls

About a mile up the road from Fowler's is a parking area around a pine tree. Park here and walk out to the overlook to see the loveliest spot on the upper river, Middle Falls, where the river makes a 40-foot drop into a deep pool.

Some anglers descend the trail below the falls to fish down to Fowler's. The fish in this area are small, wild rainbows with an occasional transient planter that worked its way upriver from Fowler's, or was washed over the falls from upriver.

Middle Falls on the McCloud. Dale Lackey

Upper Falls

About half-a-mile upstream from Middle Falls the road forks. The right fork dead ends in 3/8ths of a mile where Upper Falls descends a rocky staircase before a final cascade into the pool below.

A steep trail leads to the river and some anglers fish the half-mile portion of the river downstream to Middle Falls even though it is not a very productive stretch.

A road to the left passes an undeveloped day-use area popular with locals.

Bigelow Meadows

A half-a-mile drive ends at a locked gate on a logging bridge across the river. A deep pool under the bridge is popular with bait dunkers but fly anglers find the area less than satisfying.

The river is tightly lined with alders and willows. The only way to fish above or below the bridge would be to wade directly up the stream bed. But a silt bottom with no obvious structure makes this section unattractive as a fish holding area.

Above Bigelow Meadow Road several unimproved dirt roads lead to the river. Driving in on these roads doesn't take four-wheel drive, but in late summer the car will be enveloped in a thick cloud of dust. This part of the river has few holding areas and not many fish.

The river then cuts through a gorge of magma with boulders and plentiful vegetation, and is the most satisfying stretch on the upper river if not the best fishing. Its location is a distance from the heavily-used camping areas at Lower Falls, Upper Falls, and Cattle Camp. In a small way the character of the river in this area resembles the lower McCloud.

From here the river winds its way south away from the Loop road.

Cattle Camp

Turn right onto a dirt road at the McCloud River Loop Road sign to reach the Cattle Camp pool, a large, deep pool popular as a day use area. This area is stocked with hatchery trout on a regular basis. Continue up the McCloud River Loop Road to where it forks. Take the right fork to Angel Meadows, the last access from the Loop Road. The left fork goes to the Cattle Camp Campground and on out to intersect with Highway 89, where the McCloud River Loop Road ends.

Highway 89 Nitwit Camp—Mile 11.2

At the bottom of a draw a road to the right leads into the trees toward the river. This is an undeveloped camping area with moderately good fishing. The river is a small and shallow meandering meadow stream with some fair to good riffles interspersed with long stretches of slack water with no character.

Skunk Hollow—Mile 11.4

This is another undeveloped camping area along the river. The McCloud is a small, meandering stream in this area with little character and primarily small fish.

34

Dale Rosette fishing the upper McCloud. Dale Lackey

Four-Mile Flat—Mile 11.9

At the bottom of a dip in Highway 89 a gravel road leads to the right. This is not a marked area.

Algoma Campground—Mile 13.1

This is the uppermost access on the McCloud River. This is a developed U.S. Forest Service campground on a paved access road. The river is just a little too wide to jump across as it leaves a meadow then races over large stones and boulders through the campground. This area is planted with hatchery rainbows near the bridge on a regular basis.

The Lower McCloud River

McCloud Dam was built in the mid-1960s to divert water from the McCloud River through a tunnel to the Pit River. When the lake opened to fishing in 1966, catching a limit of 10 rainbows was simple. Fishing from a boat anchored near the lake's confluence with the river, we often caught our limit of trout by 10 a.m. and headed for home. Fishing pressure on the reservoir has made fishing very tough since then.

Before the road to Ah Di Na Campground was put through, the only way in to the lower McCloud was to pack in. The lower McCloud was the southern-most habitat for Dolly Varden, a char related to the trout family. Whenever McCloud locals hiked into Ah Di Na for a two- or three-day stay, someone in the party invariably caught a four-pound Dolly Varden, which often grew in size in the re-telling and weighed seven or eight pounds by the time the party returned home.

The McCloud Dam water diversions drastically lowered the flows of the river and consequently destroyed the deep pools necessary to the Dolly's survival. Dolly Varden haven't been documented in the McCloud River since 1975.

Angling regulations on this part of the river allow only a two fish limit from the dam downstream to Lady Bug Creek in the McCloud Preserve, and a zero limit below Lady Bug Creek.

At one time a private club, the McCloud River Club, owned the McCloud River from Ah Di Na to Shasta Lake. Some years ago, some members objected to the stiff, formal atmosphere of the club, so it was divided. The lower half of the river became the Bollibokka Club, the upper half was retained by the McCloud River Club's original members who continue to observe its traditions.

When the road to Ah Di Na made the lower Mc-Cloud accessible to the public, poaching and trespassing became a problem the McCloud River Club could not deal with. To create a buffer zone between the club property and the public they donated several miles of the uppermost property to the Nature Conservancy, an environmental organization.

Today, the Conservancy allows a controlled number of anglers onto the upper part of their river for fly fishing. The lower portion is closed to the public.

The policy of the Conservancy maintains that man is a visitor and must respect the rights of other living things to live in peace. Killing or harming any animal, even the rattlesnakes in the area, is forbidden. Those rules are made clear as you enter the property. If they offend you, go elsewhere.

As you enter the property, sign the book at the caretaker's cabin, where Conservancy volunteers are on duty. The Conservancy allows 10 anglers at a time on the property. If the spots are full, you may wait until someone leaves. On weekdays you can generally find a spot, but on weekends anglers often are turned away.

Fishing The Lower McCloud

The McCloud River has one of the most consistent flows of any stream in California. Shortly after the river leaves Fowler's Campground, mountain snow-melt gushes from springs along the river banks and is ice-cold year-round. This area, called Big Springs, is on the Hearst Estate and is closed to the public.

These flows freely tumble over the stream bed for only a few short miles. Once the river passes the lower end of the Hearst Estate it enters McCloud Reservoir. Although a minimum flow is allowed to continue down the lower McCloud past the Dam, most of the water is diverted through a tunnel toward the Pit River.

Before the road to Ah Di Na campground on the lower McCloud was opened by the U.S. Forest Service, the lower river was inaccessible unless the angler was willing to hike in.

Fred Gordon, a fishing guide living in Dunsmuir, says the McCloud is normally fishable from opening day through the end of May and can be fishable into July. With the hot weather of mid-summer, the McCloud becomes choked with glacial silt from the slopes of nearby Mount Shasta.

Conditions on the McCloud can be good earlier than on other streams because the water out of the McCloud Reservoir is regulated.

The river from the dam downstream to Ash Camp at the mouth of Hawkins Creek becomes low very early. The water gauging station is at Ah Di Na Campground, four miles downstream. Water from side streams gives the gauge enough water so that PG&E water releases into the lower McCloud must meet only minimum flows.

In mid-May the McCloud often is one of the few streams that can be fished since the others are washed out. Gordon says that "I've never seen the McCloud unfishable in all the years that I've been there. Even when it does get washed out, it doesn't stay out for long."

Beautiful brown trout caught on the McCloud. Brad Jackson

Gordon feels that the structure of the McCloud makes it a better nymph stream than a dry fly stream and recommends using dark stone fly nymphs. "Use black AP Nymphs or dark brown stones, the bigger the better. Put a couple of split shot ahead of the fly to get it down and slide an indicator up the leader to where it meets the fly line."

The lower the water, the smaller the nymph. Start with a size #8 at the beginning of the season. "The only reason I don't go bigger than that is because the bigger the fly, the more small fish I'll kill. Toward the end of the season I'll use a #16, when the fish are more finicky."

Nymph fishing can be good all day, according to Gordon, although "there is always a spot during the day when it will be best." Gordon works nymphs as though fishing a cubic piece of water rather than a surface area.

"If the water is four feet deep, divide the water into three sections—the top foot, the middle, and the bottom foot. Your first cast should be fished fast. Pick up the nymph quickly so it doesn't sink to the bottom. On the second, let the nymph work deeper. On the last cast, make sure you can feel the rocks on the bottom.

"If you fish deep first you can get snagged on the bottom," says Gordon. "By fishing the surface first, you're fishing for aggressive fish that will move for the fly.

"In the fall, watch for patches of clean gravel because big spawning browns will be on their spawning beds. Rainbows also congregate near the beds to pick up the eggs as they are spawned."

Gordon uses big stones, black AP Nymphs and black Rubberlegs. Slide the split shot down close to the nymph to make sure it bumps right down into the gravel.

Although he prefers nymphs generally, Gordon says that if fish are rising, try to match the hatch with either caddis or mayflies. "You'll want to fish very large mayflies, #6 or #8s, and some very small baetis, #16 and #18," he says.

In the early spring and late fall, look for rising fish during the warmest parts of the day. As the weather warms, the hatches will occur earlier in the morning and later in the day.

By mid-May to early June, Little Sally stone dries can be good at mid-day. By mid-June the dry fly fishing is only in the evenings, with the last hour or two of daylight the best fishing.

Gordon says to watch for large mayflies, size #6 and #8, and some small baetis, #16s and #18s.

"Elk Hair Caddis, size #14, is one of my favorite flies," says Gordon, "especially in fast water." In pools where the fish are more finicky, the imitations must be better, including using a Paradun to imitate a mayfly.

The evening dry fly activity is sporadic. Even when there is an abundance of surface activity the fish may not be moving for them.

Each stream has its most exciting time to fish and on the McCloud that time is late fall when the giant, orange caddis flies become active. These are an inch long with an orange body and folded wings in the classic caddis shape.

Three techniques are used to fish the October caddis hatch. The same fly, the Stimulator, will work for all three.

In October and November, spawning brown trout travel up the McCloud from Lake Shasta. Using streamers, fish pools early and late in the day; 18-28 inch fish are not uncommon, and double-digit leviathans are landed every year. Brad Jackson

Dead drifting the fly is the most common technique. Another is to dap the fly on the surface like a caddis laying her eggs. The third technique is to stimulate the fly with the rod tip to make it buzz or motorboat on the surface. The motorboating occurs sometime in October and only for a week when the October caddis are hatching.

Even then, Gordon prefers to use nymphs. While other anglers are intent on surface fishing the giant caddis flies, Gordon will continue nymphing with Hares' Ears, black AP Nymphs, March Browns, Stone Fly nymphs or Rubberlegs, with an indicator.

Accessing The Lower McCloud River

To reach the McCloud Reservoir and lower McCloud River, turn south off Highway 89 onto Southern Avenue, past the Shell Station, in McCloud. Follow the road through Squaw Valley then up a steep climb over a ridge and down to the reservoir.

Tarantula Gulch—Mile 9.0

The road drops from the ridge to a well-developed boat launching ramp, the only place to launch a boat on McCloud Reservoir. Follow the road to the right around the lake to reach the lower McCloud River.

Ah Di Na and the Nature Conservancy turnoff—Mile 11.3

The road to Ah Di Na and the Nature Conservancy is marked by a Forest Service sign on the right. For nearly six miles, the road winds up the ridge, overlooks the lake, then drops down to the river at Ah Di Na, a Forest Service campground.

Ah Di Na—Mile 17.2

The Forest Service campground at Ah Di Na has running water and toilets but no showers.

The McCloud Preserve—Mile 18.2

Follow the road past the campground approximately one mile to where it dead-ends. The Nature Conservancy begins at the creek at the end of the road. Cross the foot bridge and continue along a primitive trail to the Nature Conservancy cabin at Lady Bug Creek. You must sign in at a registration book on the side of the cabin. The lower McCloud is a trophy trout fisherman's dream. Riparian vegetation is abundant as the river flows over granite boulders and through long pools.

Waders will find the rocks are slick and wading can be a challenge. Felt soles or corkers are strongly advised.

Hawkins Creek—Mile 14.2

Cross the dam and turn right. After a 1.2-mile drive, a gravel road drops off to the right into an undeveloped camping area where Hawkins Creek joins the McCloud River. This is Ash Camp, where the Pacific Crest Trail crosses the McCloud River over a suspended foot bridge.

This part of the river is typical of the lower McCloud—lush plant life in a deep canyon. The river current flows very fast over large boulders. The holes aren't as well-developed as those at Ah Di Na and the Nature Conservancy.

Hawkins Creek has a small trout population, usually overlooked because accessing the river is a challenge. The rattlesnake population also tends to dampen enthusiasm for the area.

For More Information:

Fred Gordon, 6283 Gillis St., Dunsmuir, CA 96025, (916) 235-2673.

Classic pocket water and inviting pools typify the instrinsic beauty that attracts anglers to the McCloud's impatient flows. Dale Lackey

Chapter Seven

HAT CREEK

The trophy section of lower Hat Creek, probably the most famous stretch of trout water in California, provides an excellent model of what a stream can be when forces come together to make it happen.

Lower Hat Creek, that area of the stream from the Hat No. 2 Powerhouse downstream to Lake Britton, started with the potential of becoming great trout water. According to Steve Vaughn, owner of Vaughn's Sporting Goods in Burney, the stream has always had big trout. But it also had a healthy population of rough fish—suckers and squawfish that made their way into the river from Lake Britton.

In 1968, the Burney and San Francisco chapters of Trout Unlimited, the state Department of Fish and Game, Pacific Gas & Electric Co. and the Wildlife Conservation Board came together to create the first trophy trout stream in California.

A barrier dam was constructed above the stream's confluence with Lake Britton. Then the Department of Fish and Game trapped as many native trout as they could, put them in a holding pond, and poisoned the stream. With all the fish cleared out, Hat Creek was restocked with the native browns and rainbows that had been trapped.

The regulations for Hat Creek were changed, including catch restrictions and limiting tackle to artificial lures with barbless hooks. Since then, the trout population has relied on natural propagation. The stream hasn't been stocked in 20 years and today this three-mile stretch of Hat Creek is one of the most popular pieces of water in the state.

Baum Lake

Baum Lake deserves a mention of its own. It is a PG&E impoundment—water comes into Baum Lake

Dale Lackey

through Powerhouse 1 from the Cassel Forebay and leaves through Powerhouse 2, into lower Hat Creek.

Steve Vaughn suggests fishing Baum Lake as if it were a wide spot in Hat Creek; it has the same insect patterns and the fish respond to the same lures, flies and bait as the stream. The lake is a buffer zone between upper Hat Creek, a heavily-stocked, put-and-take fishery, and the lower Hat Creek trophy section.

Bait anglers find salmon eggs, crawlers, crickets and Power Bait effective. Spin fishermen use blade lures—Panther Martins, Kastmasters, Rooster Tails or Mepps.

During the winter, insects may become active during warm periods, but bait is the only consistent way to take fish.

The lake is shallow, about 30 feet. Fly fishermen use float tubes or prams to get onto the lake. They fish midge nymphs, black or gray, Gold Ribbed Hare's Ears, Sawyer's PT Nymphs, or streamers such as matukas or leech patterns in black, olive, or brown. Fish these patterns with a sink tip line, retrieving with short twitches along the bottom.

Upper Hat Creek

Hat Creek begins as a tumbling mountain stream on the slopes of Hat Peak in Lassen Volcanic National Park. It leaves the park near Old Station, passing through a number of campgrounds that are part of Lassen National Forest. Then it enters the fertile bottomland of the Hat Creek Valley, where it becomes a meandering meadow stream.

Near the tiny community of Cassel, Hat Creek is joined by Rising River. Rising River is a true spring creek, clear water bubbling from valley springs and winding across the valley floor over a bed of limestone. In essence, at their

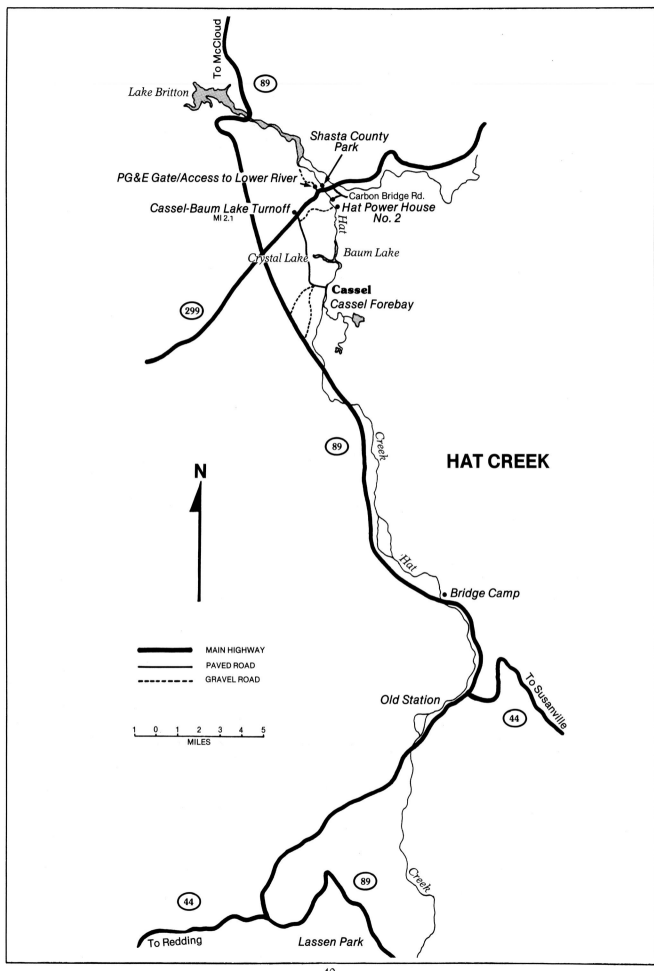

To McCloud

89

Lake Britton

Shasta County Park

PG&E Gate/Access to Lower River

Carbon Bridge Rd.

Cassel-Baum Lake Turnoff

MI 2.1

Hat Power House No. 2

Hat

Crystal Lake

Baum Lake

Cassel

Cassel Forebay

299

N

89

Creek

HAT CREEK

Hat

MAIN HIGHWAY
PAVED ROAD
GRAVEL ROAD

1 0 1 2 3 4 5
MILES

• *Bridge Camp*

To Susanville

Old Station

44

89

Creek

44

To Redding

Lassen Park

confluence Hat Creek becomes Rising River in every way except name.

At the Cassel Forebay, or Cassel Intake, the stream goes through Hat 1 Powerhouse and empties into Baum Lake. It leaves Baum Lake through a diversion then re-enters the river channel at the Hat No. 2 Powerhouse.

The Trophy Trout Section of Hat Creek begins at the Hat 2 Powerhouse and runs downstream to where the stream enters Lake Britton.

Fishing Upper Hat Creek

Hat Creek is accessible to the public where it follows Highway 44 from Big Pine Campground downstream to Old Station, then follows Highway 89 to Bridge Campground. From there it enters private property where access is not allowed. The only other public access is at Honn Campground.

This upper part of Hat Creek is not a blue-ribbon stream. It is heavily stocked and fished, typical baitfishing water where the quality of fishing is directly related to the last visit by the hatchery truck.

On the other hand, there are no special regulations or pretensions. A kid with a spinning rod and a jar of salmon eggs can be just as successful as a veteran fly angler.

Where Hat Creek leaves the national forest it enters private property and access to the stream is severely restricted.

Lower Hat Creek

From the Cassel Forebay to the Hat 2 Powerhouse Inlet, on Baum Lake and Crystal Lake, there are no special fishing regulations.

"Fishing in this area can be dynamite," says Steve Vaughn. A few years ago, Vaughn caught a 24-inch, seven-pound rainbow in the Cassel Forebay on a #16 Adams.

Fly fishing isn't all that works in this area. Bait anglers use crickets, night crawlers, salmon eggs and Power Bait as effectively as fly anglers use nymphs and dries. Lures also work well, including Panther Martins, Kastmasters or small Rapalas.

Fly fishing the Cassel Forebay and Baum Lake is much the same as fishing the flat water of lower Hat Creek. Fish stonefly nymphs in the early season, then switch to the smaller pale morning duns, pale evening duns and caddis when the weather warms.

There are no gear restrictions and the limit follows general state regulations. Fishing can be dynamite, although not all fish are trophy-size.

The Trophy Trout Section

The Trophy Trout section of Hat Creek is between the Hat Creek 2 Powerhouse and Lake Britton.

This section of Hat Creek, the most famous piece of trout water in California, is a fly fisherman's dream. It's also a fly fisherman's nightmare, with its multiple hatches and clear water. In addition, it has the characteristics of two

Angling success on Hat Creek largely depends on a perfect, drag-free drift. Lazy flows and a characteristically glass-smooth surface dictate the use of micro-tippets and slack-line presentations. Dale Lackey

separate streams—one section is a flat-water spring creek, the other section is a free-stone stream with shallow riffles.

"In the space of an hour you can see four different flies hatch," says Duane Milleman, a Redding guide who has fished the area for years. "You will see one type of insect hatch out and think you have it nailed. Fifteen minutes later the fish will feed on something else.

"Two or three sizes and colors of mayflies will come off at the same time," continues Milleman. "Normally, the trout will key on the smallest size insect because of the biomass—there are more of them."

Autumn brings gorgeous color transition to Lower Hat Creek's riparian zone of mixed hardwoods. Indian summer days permit civilized angling shifts, with surface action principally occuring from late morning to early afternoon. Brad Jackson

Early Season Fishing
"The salmon fly hatch is the big draw at the opening of trout season," Milleman says. "In years past it was over before the season started, but sometimes now it doesn't even come off until June."

There are two species of early stoneflies, the big golden stones and salmon flies. The big golden stones come off first and may be active on the opening day of trout season in some years. In other years they may not become active until May.

The golden stones gradually give way to pteronarcys, the big salmon flies. "I've seen salmon flies come off clear into June," says Milleman, "and I've even seen a second emergence of salmon flies in July. Although it isn't well known, it does happen."

Green drakes hatch in May or June, and some years they come off during both months. Green drakes like cold, blustery, spitting-rain days in the early season.

Begin fishing each hatch with nymphs. The nymphs become active first, then become emergers, which come to the surface before the fly leaves the water. It is the adult fly which is imitated by a dry. Adults sit on the surface of the water while their wings dry and take shape before they are able to fly.

Stoneflies are different. Instead of rising to the sur-

face as an emerger, they crawl out of the water onto rocks or vegetation at the edge of the stream.

Hat Creek has flies active at some stage or another all the time. As nymphs, they come out from under the rocks and feed on algae two or three times a day. Anglers will start hammering the fish for no apparent reason, then the bite will shut off. This is determined by water temperature and it works differently on every stream.

But when stonefly nymphs start migrating toward the shore, the fishing can really turn on.

The dry fly action on these big stones is early in the year, "but the nymphs are in the water year-round," says Milleman. "You can catch fish in riffle water with big nymph imitations all the time. The only difference is that after a hatch the big nymphs are gone and you will want to drop down a size or so."

In May, the pale morning dun mayfly hatches begin on the flat water of Hat Creek. These hatches are sporadic, but the heaviest activity occurs in June.

There is also a pale evening dun. They are very similar to the pale morning dun, except that they hatch in the evening and late evening.

To sum up, in the early season watch for the stoneflies, green drakes, pale morning duns and pale evening duns. The hatches intensify into June, then fade as July approaches. The hatches become compressed to earlier in the morning and later in the evening as the days become warmer.

Mid-Season
As warm weather approaches—late June, July and August— the hatches of large stoneflies fade and the pale morning and pale evening duns compress into very early morning and very late evening.

It's then the smaller insects become active on Hat Creek. There's a very small baetis, the blue-wing olive, that becomes prevalent, along with the trico.

In the mornings during July and August, fish the trico spinner fall in the flat water below Powerhouse 2 and in the evenings fish the trico hatch.

Little yellow stones begin hatching in June, peaking in July. The hatch occurs at the end of a normal warm day but can go on all day during cloudy weather. It occurs intermittently throughout summer and peaks again in the fall.

Steve Vaughn of Vaughn's Sporting Goods suggests that anglers fish little yellow stone nymphs or emergers during the hatch, then perhaps switch to dries in the evening.

In July, the pale morning dun hatches are still sputtering in July at the Powerhouse riffle.

"The trico fall on Hat Creek can be really rewarding for those who can handle long, light leaders and a small fly," says Milleman. "It's really difficult fishing, but it's wonderful."

Caddis flies also are active on Hat Creek, which can be confusing. Hat Creek has a micro-caddis, little creatures, #20s and #22s, so small sometimes you can't see them. They're in the surface film and anglers swear there is no hatch, except that they can see fish feeding everywhere.

"Evenings can be an absolute mind blower," says

"The fast water" above Lake Britton contains verdant landscapes, sexy pocket water, and the opportunity for challenging wading and short-line nymphing.
Brad Jackson

Milleman. "Mayflies are coming and going, and caddis flies are starting. Sometimes this is compressed into the last half hour of the day. For the rest of the day you are left to your own devices with nymphs or terrestrials—ants, beetles, or grasshoppers," says Milleman. "Terrestrials are good if you can find an area where fish are stacked up along the edge of the stream."

Fall

As the weather begins to cool in late September and October, the baetis hatch becomes very intense and the pale morning dun becomes active again.

The biggest fall fly hatch to occur on Hat Creek is the October caddis. This hatch used to occur in unbelievable numbers on Hat Creek. They were so prolific the boots of fishermen walking in the shallows crunched on the discarded nymph cases. It's still good, but those days are gone.

Fly Patterns

Early Season: Golden Stone nymphs and dries, #4 and #6; Salmon Flies #2 to #4 (use a size or two smaller nymph the rest of the season); Green Drakes, #10 and #12 for both nymphs and dries.

Mid-season (July through September): Pale Morning Dun, Pale Evening Dun, Trico and Caddis, #14 to #22 in about 3 colors; Little Yellow Stones, #16.

Late Season (October and November): Pale Morning Dun, Blue Wing Olives, Baetis and October Caddis; Small Caddis #16 to #18, Baetis, Pale Evening Dun with a Light Olive, #16 to #18.

Access

The junction of Highways 299 and 89 will be the point of origin for Hat Creek access routes.

Mile 0.0

The junction of Highways 299 and 89 can be reached two ways. Take the Highway 299 East exit from Interstate 5 just north of Redding (don't be confused by the Highway 299 West Exit about 2 miles to the south) and follow Highway 299 east to Burney. Two miles past Burney, Highway 299 intersects with Highway 89 at the Outpost Restaurant and Motel.

Another route further to the north is to take Highway 89 at the McCloud Exit of I-5, just south of Mount Shasta City. Follow Highway 89 east through the town of McCloud and on about 50 miles to the Highway 299-Highway 89 intersection. A left turn on to Highway 299 goes north to lower Hat Creek, a right turn goes to Burney. Straight ahead will take you to upper Hat Creek.

Cassel

Mile 2.1—Cassel-Baum Lake turnoff

The Cassel Road leads to the Cassel Forebay, Baum Lake and Crystal Lake.

Turn right onto Cassel Road. The Baum Lake/Crystal Creek Hatchery is 2.1 miles along Cassel Road. Turn left and drive one mile to the hatchery. Baum Lake is to the left with a large parking area.

At mile 3.5 Cassel Road crosses Hat Creek at the Cassel Forebay. A camping and parking area on the left parallels the channel of the Forebay.

The Trophy Trout Section

Mile 2.7—Hat Creek Powerhouse No. 2

From the junction of Highways 89 and 299, continue north 2.7 miles to a road on the right marked "Hat No. 2." This is the PG&E access road to Hat Creek Powerhouse No. 2. At this point the water is diverted from Baum Lake to the Powerhouse.

At the parking area near the powerhouse, a sign in a kiosk describes the efforts that went into creating California's first trophy-trout stream.

The first piece of water is the Powerhouse Riffle. Below that it has the classic character of a spring creek with long, flat pools. It winds its way through the rolling hills in banks lined with cat-tails and tall grass, a rich contrast to the dry, rolling hills that surround Hat Creek.

This is the Hat Creek that challenges the angler head on, requiring long, gossamer leaders and perfect, drag-free, dead drift dry fly presentations or nymph fishing with indicators.

Mile 3.4—PG&E Gate

This offers access to the riffle section, the barrier dam and the stream's confluence with Lake Britton.

On the left side of Highway 299, a green metal gate marks the PG&E access road to the lower river. Several side roads lead off, but bearing to the right for 0.7 mile leads to a fork in the road. Take the right fork onto a meadow and another fence. A path through a gate leads downriver, a fork to the right ends at another fence. Park here to fish upriver.

The riffle section runs from just above the fence downstream to the barrier dam. From the fence upstream to the county park the stream has little character. Fish in this area hide beneath undercut banks or around the occasional fallen tree that is buried in the limestone silt.

Mile 3.7—Shasta County Picnic Area

Although fishing is legal at the Shasta County Park and picnic area, few people seem to bother.

This part of the stream is like the others, a limestone stream bed covered with aquatic weeds. One can sit at one of the picnic tables enjoying a cold drink on a warm summer evening and watch trout rise for an endless variety of mayflies and caddis.

Mile 3.8—Bridge over Hat Creek

A short distance past the Shasta County Park is a cattle pen and loading chute on the right side of Highway 299. The road to the upper section of Hat Creek goes through the gate, past the pen and winds away from the stream.

Mile 4.2—Carbon Bridge Road

Bear to the right and you will come to the parking area at the old Carbon Bridge. Here, Hat Creek meanders over a limestone bed choked with aquatic weeds. The stream is undisturbed by boulders.

For More Information:

Duane Milleman, The Fly Shop Outfitters, 4140 Churn Creek Rd., Redding, CA 96002, (916) 243-5317. • Steve Vaughn, Vaughn's Sporting Goods, P.O. Box 2690, Burney, CA 96013, (916) 335-2381.

Shy Hat Creek brown trout prefer shady lies beneath overhanging trees and next to cut banks and snags. It takes sharp eyes to spot the subtle rises and accurate casts to deliver the dry fly down the feeding lane. Brad Jackson

Chapter Eight

TRINITY RIVER

The Trinity River is included in this book to make anglers aware of the historic and potential greatness of the stream. With a little care and a great deal of political pressure, the Trinity can recover its former greatness and again become a blue ribbon trout fishery.

The Trinity's history as a trout stream centers around its brown trout population. For years, anglers flocked to the Trinity in the spring to fish for trophy-sized, sea-run brown trout. Whether they fished with lures, bait or flies, they made consistent catches of 4- to 12-pound browns.

Brown trout are not native to North America—they were brought here from Europe in the late 19th Century in exchange for rainbow trout. The browns brought to the Trinity were the Loch Leven variety from Scotland rather than the German browns now common in the Western United States.

Loch Leven browns are called sea trout in Europe because they are anadromous, like steelhead. Hatching from eggs in the river, they go to sea for a year or more, enjoying the rich food supply of the ocean and growing much faster than they would in fresh water. Ultimately, however, they return to the stream to spawn as trophy-sized fish.

When Trinity Dam was built in 1961, several hundred miles of prime spawning habitat was closed to salmon, steelhead and Loch Leven browns. As the lake behind the dam began to fill, the flows in the Trinity River were reduced to 150 cubic feet per second.

Without normal flows to flush silt out of the stream bed, gravel in the lower Trinity became cemented, making spawning difficult.

Salmon and steelhead were reduced to near extinc-

Brad Jackson.

tion, but browns were maintained as a stocked fishery. Since they are cannibalistic foragers, they ate anything in sight, including the juvenile salmon and steelhead. This made them a scapegoat for the water agencies, who blamed the browns for the low salmon and steelhead runs, ignoring the loss of habitat and low flows as a cause.

The brown trout stocking program was halted in 1978 but the browns continued to flourish until the early 1980s, when they began to decline.

The Trinity's brown trout today are remnants that have become resident river fish. The population is very low, only about 26 fish to the mile according to a recent survey. But they hang on and provide fishing for anglers willing to work for them.

Unfortunately for the brown trout population, those anglers who catch the big fish—the spawners—tend to kill them rather than practice catch and release.

The tributaries of the Trinity above Trinity Lake also offer good trout fishing in the spring and fall. Trout from the lake enter Coffee Creek, the Stuart's Fork and the other major tributaries to spawn, some in the spring, others in the fall.

The construction of the two dams on the river did benefit anglers in other ways. Lewiston Lake and Trinity Lake—officially Clair Engle Lake, but don't call it that in Trinity County—have become fine fisheries in their own right.

Trinity Lake has excellent bass fishing, as well as kokanee and trout. In fact, the state record smallmouth bass was caught in Trinity Lake.

Lewiston Reservoir, the flow regulation dam below Trinity Lake, has splendid trout fishing of a different nature.

Trinity River
(Lewiston Dam to the Klamath)

Fishing Techniques

Flies: The Trinity River immediately below Lewiston Dam is a fly-fishing only area that extends to the Old Lewiston Bridge.

Herb Burton, owner of Trinity Alps Fly Shop and Guide Service in Lewiston, has been fishing the Trinity River system for a quarter century. Burton has fished from the alpine lakes that feed the tributaries of the Trinity to its confluence with the Klamath River.

Burton says the brown trout population extends from Lewiston to Del Loma, about 40 miles downstream, but the bulk of the fish are concentrated in the upper 20 miles, above Junction City.

Early in the season, the hatchery releases juvenile salmon and steelhead into the river just below Lewiston Dam, and for a time the waters boil with these tiny fish. The browns have a feast until these small fish move downstream and out of that stretch of water. Burton says anglers should use streamers that simulate steelhead or salmon fry in the fly fishing section while the juveniles are present.

The river also has a substantial population of lamprey eels so dark leech patterns such as Woolly Buggers, and Olive or Black Matukas will work as imitations of small eels.

When the season opens, little golden stones populate the tail water of the pools. Use golden stone imitations in #8s through #12s. The Lewiston area also has salmon flies (Pteronarcys californica), but further downriver anglers will encounter fewer of these giant stoneflies.

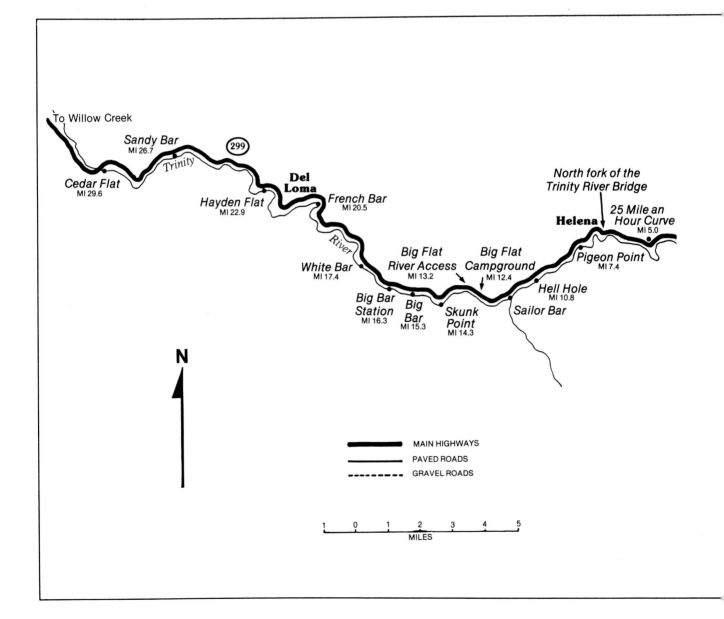

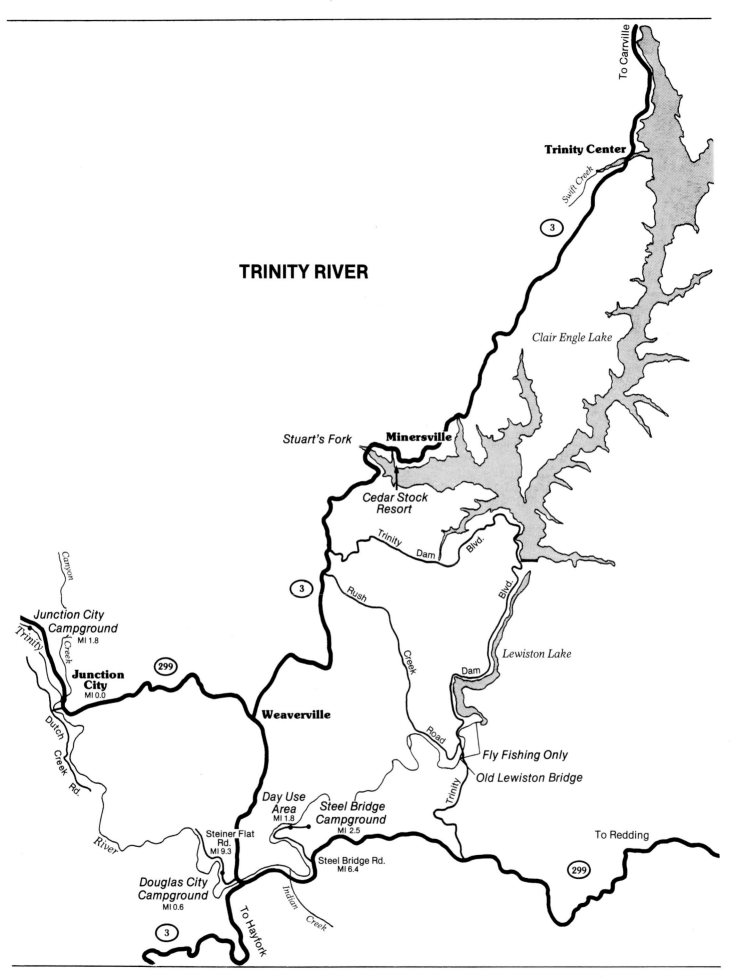

TRINITY RIVER

To Carrville

Trinity Center

Swift Creek

③

Clair Engle Lake

Stuart's Fork

Minersville

Cedar Stock Resort

Trinity   Dam   Blvd.

Blvd.

Lewiston Lake

Dam

Rush

Creek

③

Canyon

Junction City Campground
MI 1.8

Trinity

Creek

Junction City
MI 0.0

(299)

Weaverville

Road

Trinity

Fly Fishing Only

Old Lewiston Bridge

Dutch

Creek

Rd.

Day Use Area
MI 1.8

Steel Bridge Campground
MI 2.5

To Redding

River

Steiner Flat Rd.
MI 9.3

Steel Bridge Rd.
MI 6.4

(299)

Douglas City Campground
MI 0.6

③

To Hayfork

Indian   Creek

Stark hardwoods act as sentinels while an angler prospects for steelhead.
Brad Jackson

Early in the season, streamers generally will take the biggest fish. Most run from 14 to 19 inches, but occasionally six to eight pounders are caught. As the season progresses, golden stone nymph imitations become the most productive, fished dead and deep.

In late summer, an intense but brief caddis hatch occurs late in the evenings. The most common is the gray caddis that's indigenous to almost every river system in the West, but there also is an olive caddis hatch.

Fish the caddis hatch with caddis nymphs and what Burton calls Dirty Black Emergers (DBEs). When fish obviously take adult caddis off the surface, fish Elk Hair Caddis dries.

At this time of year, streamers fished in the late evening and early morning also are productive.

Lures and Bait: Below the Old Lewiston Bridge, the lower boundary of the fly fishing only section of the river, lures catch more browns than flies or bait.

The most effective lures are back-trolled Hot Shots and Wee Warts, which catch browns while being fished by drift boat anglers for salmon or steelhead.

Bank anglers can fish spinners, either Panther Martins or Little Cleos. Fish these by casting the lure across the river and letting it swing across the current, then retrieving it upstream along the seam between the main current and the eddy along the bank. Or cast upstream and retrieve quickly downstream past the boulders that line the head of the pool.

Bait fishermen catch most of the browns while fishing the deep pools for salmon or steelhead. Although salmon anglers have better luck fishing the Trinity with tuna balls, an occasional brown is caught on salmon or steelhead roe.

Night crawlers are also a good bait for browns. Artificial baits, such as Power Bait, do not work as well.

Access

Highway 299 is the main corridor for access to the Trinity River. Secondary accesses take off from Highway 299, such as Lewiston Road, Steel Bridge Road and Steiner Flat Road. Each area will be identified as directly accessible from Highway 299, or from one of the secondary accesses.

The Upper Trinity River
Lewiston to Douglas City
Highway 299—Mile 0.0
Trinity Dam Blvd. Secondary Access

This is the uppermost access from Highway 299 and all other accesses will be in relation to the Lewiston Road exit from Highway 299.

Access to the upper river is from the first Lewiston Exit, 28 miles west of Redding on Highway 299. This is about 4 miles west of Buckhorn Summit.

Turn right and follow Trinity Dam Blvd. 6.4 miles, through the town of Lewiston, to the bridge that crosses the river.

Mile 6.4—Trinity Dam Blvd.
The Fly Fishing Only Section.

This is the uppermost section of the main river. Instead of crossing the bridge, turn right onto Hatchery Road. The fly-fishing only section begins 0.3 mile up Hatchery Road and extends downstream to the Old Lewiston Bridge. This area is filled with long, fast-moving shallow riffles. Migrating salmon and steelhead hold from here up to the dam and the hatchery entrance.

Old Lewiston Bridge

Cross the bridge and turn left onto Rush Creek Road. The Old Lewiston Bridge is 0.7 mile downstream from the first bridge and is a picturesque, suspended one-lane span. Next to the bridge is a fishing access, boat-launch and parking area. The river is wide and flat but holds fish during the steelhead and salmon migrations.

Rush Creek Fishing Access

About two miles farther down Rush Creek Road is a developed fishing access, boat launch and parking area. This access is about 100 yards long and provides wading and boat access to several good pools. This is the last public access along the river until Steel Bridge Campground.

Mile 6.4—Highway 299
Steel Bridge Road

Steel Bridge Road is a paved side road off Highway 299 that provides a few accesses to the river as well as a launch or pull-out access for boaters.

Mile 1.8—Steel Bridge Road
Day use area

Turn right, follow Steel Bridge Road 1.8 miles to a day-use area next to the river.

Mile 2.2—Steel Bridge Road
Day Use Area

Follow Steel Bridge Road to a flat and gravel bar area next to an old bridge foundation.

Mile 2.5—Steel Bridge Road
Steel Bridge Campground

Follow Steel Bridge Road 2.5 miles to the campground at the end of the road.

From mile 6.8 to Douglas City, the Trinity River follows Highway 299 and in some areas the river can be accessed by parking next to the road and walking in to the river. The area does have some residences along it so be sure not to trespass to get to the river.

Mile 7.7—Highway 299
Indian Creek

On the west side of Indian Creek, across from the Indian Creek Motel, a gravel road leads to an undeveloped area next to the river. This has several good fishing pools and boat anglers can launch or load their boats from the gravel bar.

Across the road from the river is Indian Creek Trailer Park, a private campground and RV Park.

Mile 9.3—Highway 299 Steiner Flat Road

Douglas City Mile 0.0—Steiner Flat Road
Steiner Flat Road and Highway 89

Cross the bridge and turn into Douglas City, bear to the left to Steiner Flat Road.

Mile 0.6—Steiner Flat Road
BLM Campground

The campground entrance is on a hill 0.6 mile down the road.

Mile 1.8—Steiner Flat Road
Undeveloped parking area

There is an undeveloped parking area next to the road. The river has deep pools flowing through alder-lined banks. Getting to the river is the easy part, fishing among the alders and willows is tough for fly anglers. Spin fishermen will find it much easier.

Mile 2.0—Steiner Flat Road Pavement ends

Mile 2.6—Steiner Flat Road Pavement resumes

Mile 2.8—Steiner Flat Road
Road to the river

A road to the left leads down to a flat area along the river. Another road follows the gravel bar along the river for several hundred yards.

After dismal escapement in the late seventies, Trinity River steelhead are making a comeback. Biologists credit increased flows mandated by the Carter Administration, habitat rehabilitation, and better methods at Trinity River Hatchery. Brad Jackson

Mile 3.9—Steiner Flat Road
Lazy L Mine

A bridge crosses a tiny creek and turns left to the river. This is a private mining claim.

Mile 4.1—Steiner Flat Road
Pavement ends

The pavement ends here. It is a good idea to stop here and turn around. A locked gate blocks the road at mile 4.5, which is not a good place to turn around.

Mile 13.6—Highway 299
Weaverville
Mile 14.2—Highway 299

Junction of Highway 299 and Highway 3 in Weaverville

Weaverville is a picturesque community with a mining past. It has lodging, restaurants and excellent fishing information at Brady's Tackle Shop located in the Weaverville Hotel.

The Trinity carves its way through a precipitous canyon as it flows west along Highway 299. In the background, fresh snow dresses the Trinity Alps Range that feeds the river's flows. Brad Jackson

The Lower Trinity River

For the purposes of this book, the lower Trinity River runs from Junction City to Cedar Flat.

Mile 0.0—Highway 299
Junction City

Mile 0.3—Highway 299
Dutch Creek Road

Dutch Creek Road crosses the Trinity and goes upstream about four miles. The road ends at a gravel bar that runs along the river.

Mile 0.6—Highway 299
Canyon Creek

A gravel bar follows the river from the other side, but on the highway side, the pools must be accessed by climbing down directly from the road.

Mile 1.8—Highway 299
Junction City Campground

This is a USFS campground next to the highway and about 200 yards from the river. A good but undeveloped road leads to the river. This is an excellent area for launching or pulling out a boat or raft.

Mile 4.0—Highway 299
Bigfoot RV Park

This is a private resort on the river offering camping and RV spaces.

Mile 5.0—Highway 299
25-Mile-an-hour highway curve

A gravel road at the downstream end of the curve provides access to several hundred yards of gravel bar. Anglers can launch or pull out a boat, or access the river by foot from the gravel bar.

Mile 5.4—Highway 299
Elk Horn Lodge

A private resort with cabins, camping, RV spaces and guide service.

Mile 7.0—Highway 299
North Fork Bridge

This bridge crosses the North Fork of the Trinity at its confluence with the main river. There is an undeveloped launch area below the bridge.

A road, (Forest Service 34N07) follows the North Fork up to Old Helena, an abandoned town. It follows the North Fork for several miles.

Access to the North Fork is very difficult and it is not noted as a trout fishery. It is a prime spawning stream and most of its fish are juvenile steelhead or salmon.

Special regulations apply to this stream—only fish under 14 inches may be kept.

Mile 7.4—Highway 299
Pigeon Point

Pigeon Point is a USFS campground on the banks of the Trinity River. It is a fishing access as well as a launch site for rafters and kayakers. Drift boaters are warned not to run the river between here and Big Flat.

Several popular pools for salmon and steelhead anglers are between Pigeon Point and Big Flat, including Hells Drop, probably the most popular fishing spot between Junction City and Cedar Flat.

Mile 10.8—Highway 299
Hell Hole

Hells Hole is an eight-foot waterfall and one of the best salmon holding pools on the river. It is also an exciting ride for rafters and kayakers. About one-tenth of a mile downstream is a long parking area.

Mile 12.4—Highway 299
Big Flat Campground

Big Flat Campground, located a short distance up Wheel Gulch Road, is a USFS campground opposite the river, just upstream from the community of Big Flat.

Mile 12.7—Highway 299
Fishtail Inn and Steelhead Cottages

This is a bar and restaurant with cabins nearby. Fishtail Rapid is the last major rapid on the river before rafters pull out at Big Flat River Access.

Mile 12.9—Highway 299
Trinity River Inn

This is a store with gas pumps and a small restaurant. It has a private campground and RV park. Launching is allowed at the campground, probably for a fee. Because policies often change on private property, ask for permission in the store before launching.

Mile 13.2—Highway 299
Big Flat River Access

This is a parking area with a trail to the river. River runners use this as an exit point from the river after running the gorge. You can walk to the river, but cannot drive a car.

Mile 14.3—Highway 299
Skunk Point

This is a USFS campground and day use area on the river.

This is the head of Trinity Lake from the high French Gulch Road. True headwaters of the Trinity River are on the westward slope of the Trinity Divide. Frank Raymond

Mile 15.3—Highway 299
Big Bar Ranger Station

A road, with an unimproved river access, crosses the river near the Big Bar Ranger Station.

Mile 16.3—Highway 299
Big Bar Station

This resort area has a store and restaurant.

Mile 17.4—Highway 299
Whites Bar

This is a USFS day use area on the river.

Mile 20.5—Highway 299
French Bar

A gravel road leads to the gravel bar that runs a considerable distance along the river.

Mile 20.5—Highway 299
Big French Creek

Big French Creek flows into the Trinity from the north side of the river. A large hole below the confluence is a popular fishing spot for salmon and steelhead anglers.

Mile 21.4—Highway 299
Del Loma

This is a private resort area with a campground and RV camping. A short distance upriver from Del Loma is a road that leads into the gravel bar and provides access to the river above the residences in Del Loma.

Mile 22.9—Highway 299
Hayden Flat

Hayden Flat is a USFS campground on both sides of the highway.

Mile 26.7—Highway 299
Sandy Bar

This is a USFS day-use area and Trinity River Access point.

Mile 29.6—Highway 299
Cedar Flat

One the upriver side of the bridge is a day-use area as well as a warning to boaters. The river enters Burnt Ranch Gorge and in the next several miles becomes one of the most challenging stretches of white water in the West.

From Cedar Flat downstream to the Trinity's confluence with the Klamath, the Trinity is no longer a trout stream, although it can have excellent salmon and steelhead fishing.

The river enters Burnt Ranch Gorge, a heavy class V whitewater river. From here downstream to Hawkins Bar, special regulations may apply so consult the current DFG fishing rules.

For More Information:
Trinity River:

Herb Burton, Trinity Alps Anglers, P.O. Box 176, Lewiston, CA 96052, (916) 623-6757. • Tim Brady, Brady's Sport Shop, 201 Main Street, Weaverville, CA 96093, (916) 623-3121. Joe Mercier, Trinity Canyon Lodge, P.O. Box 51, Junction City, CA 96048, (916) 623-6318.

Trinity Lake:

Steve Johannsen, Cedar Stock Resort, Star Route, Box 510, Lewiston, CA 96052, (916) 286-2555.

Lewiston Lake:

Herb Burton, Trinity Alps Anglers, P.O. Box 176, Lewiston, CA 96052, (916) 623-6757. • Herb VanDerwall, Lakeview Terrace Resort, Star Route, Box 250, Lewiston, CA 96052, (916) 778-3808.

The water immediately below Lewiston Dam to the Old Lewiston Iron Bridge is open to artificial flies with barbless hooks from the last Saturday in April to September 15. Frank Raymond

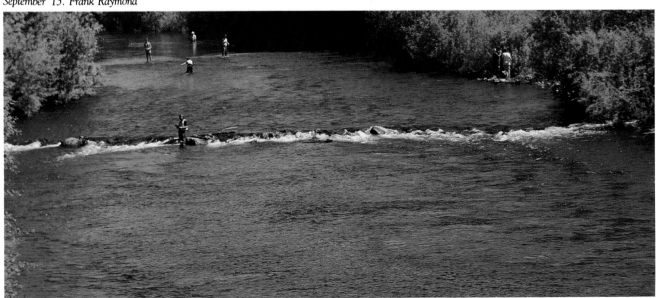

Chapter Nine

FALL RIVER

Those of us who fish Fall River probably are drawn there solely for the amusement of the stream's trophy rainbows.

The trout have seen thousands of man-crafted insects through the gin-clear water and by the end of May they have little trouble identifying the artificial flies with real hooks from the real flies with no hooks.

Success on Fall River is measured in degrees, not numbers. It's how close you come to landing a fish. Getting the fly into a perfect, drag-free drift is step one. Keeping an eye on the fly is stage two, and so on, until a rainbow is fought to the boat and released.

The numbers of fish hooked aren't high, but the stakes are. The satisfaction is in having a shot at a trophy fish—like going a couple of rounds with a champion.

Fall River is a spring creek, emerging from the ground at Thousand Springs and then winding its way across the Fall River Valley toward the town of Fall River, where penstocks carry it to Pit River Powerhouse #1 on the Pit River.

Fall River isn't a public stream. It is surrounded by private ranchers who don't allow anglers to cross their land. The Fall River Decision was a landmark in California access law.

Ranchers used to build fences across the river to keep boaters from fishing behind their property. A lawsuit that went through the California court system finally was decided by the state Supreme Court. The decision was that the public has the right to use, unimpeded, a navigable stream and the landowners were forced to pull their fences out of the river.

However, the courts did not say that the public had the right to cross private property to reach the stream.

Cal Trout acquired an access next to the Island Road Bridge on the middle section of the river and will allow a limited number of anglers to launch there. Rick's Lodge and the Fly Shop Outfitters offer access across their property for a fee.

Dale Lackey

Anglers used to slide their boats into the river at a site near the Glenburn Church where the river abuts the road. But that site was closed off when a landowner put a fence along the road.

The stream isn't waded because there's no place to wade that isn't on private property. Fishing has to be done by casting from a boat, usually a pram powered by an electric motor.

Access is available at the three sites mentioned above, and these are for boat launching only. But once on the river, the length of it is yours.

The clear water of Fall River requires a finicky approach to fishing for its 18- to 20-inch average rainbows and browns. Leaders are by necessity light, 2- or 3-pound test, and long, 12 to 17 feet.

Fortunately, Fall River is blessed with exceptional fishing guides, including Duane Milleman, who has fished the river since 1964.

Flies are presented in a downstream dead-drift known to fly fishers as "The Fall River Drift." Anchor a pram above a pod of rising fish and select just one fish to cast to. Most of the time you will be casting a #16 paradun or a #18 to #20 trico imitation.

Choose a spot above the working fish where the current will carry the fly into its feeding zone. Cast so that the fly lands well above the fish and past his feeding lane. Then drag the line to straighten the leader and draw the fly in line with the feeding fish.

As the fly drifts toward the fish, pile line loosely on the water so the fly passes drag-free over the fish. As soon as the fly is past the feeding zone, pull it away. Do not let the fly line go over the fish, it will put them down the rest of the day.

Milleman divides the upper Fall River, from the river's origin at Thousand Springs to the Tule River, into three sections, each with its own characteristics.

The upper third of the river, from Thousand Springs

to Spring Creek bridge, is the only section with trees.

When fishing season opens the last Saturday in April, the action in this area is dominated by pale morning dun mayflies. Milleman recommends a #16 tan paradun, or an olive or sulfur dun for the hatch, which occurs in the morning. Switch to an Olive Quill Spinner for the spinner fall later in the day.

According to Milleman, the hatch gradually builds through May and peaks in late June, then tapers off as summer approaches. In late September it begins to peak again.

On almost any windy, blustery day in late spring or early fall, it is possible to see large, olive-green mayflies on the water. These are green drakes.

According to former Fall River guide Andy Burk, the green drake hatch is seldom active enough to create any great excitement. "But," says Burk, "once a trout eats a green drake, he never lets another one go by." Burk came to that conclusion when a rainbow he had fished over for several days rose for a passing green drake. He caught the same fish on three consecutive evenings on a green drake pattern.

In late June, blue wing olives (baetis mayflies) become active. "The spinner fall occurs only on the upper river, in the trees," says Milleman. "In years past, fish migrated into the upper river for the spinner fall."

But the weed growth in the upper river isn't as prolific as it once was. "This hasn't hindered the fishing, it just changes where we fish," Milleman says.

Now the trout tend to stack up in the middle river around Spring Creek Bridge. "The weed growth in this area is phenomenal," says Milleman.

During the hot summer months, the trico spinner fall is incredible. These #18 to #22 flies continue to create action right into fall.

On and off hatches continue into the summer months. Dry fly fishing can be excellent even on days when the mercury climbs above 100—incredibly big fish rise for dries around Island Road Bridge, usually between 11 a.m. and 2 p.m.

The lower third of the Fall River is from Island Road Bridge to the Tule River. At this time, the Cal Trout Access at Island Road Bridge is the lowest public access to the river.

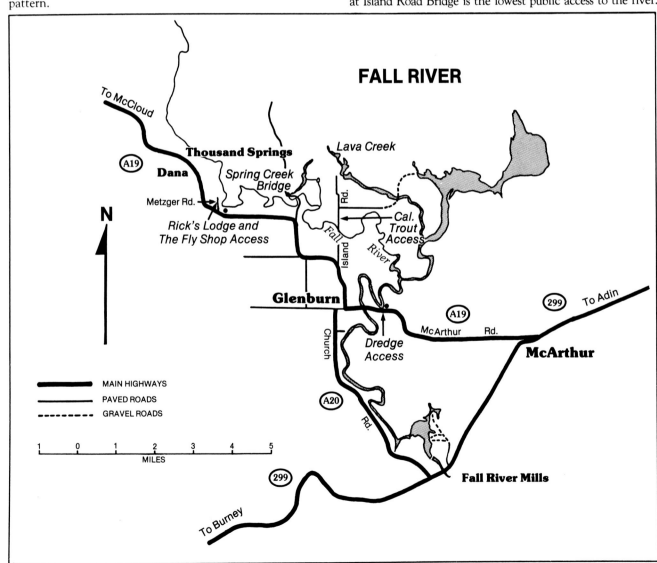

Colorful trees framed against nearby Soldier Mountain. Frank Raymond

Caddis hatches begin in late June or early July and intensify into August. "If there were a time that I'd guarantee someone a fish, it would be evenings in mid to late summer with caddis dries or caddis pupa," says Milleman. "The best and most predictable hatches of the season are at that time of year. As fall approaches, the caddis and trico hatches slow down. Then in September, the baetis mayflies—blue wing olives—and the pale morning duns become more active."

Milleman says if the fish aren't taking dries, try a PT Nymph or similar pattern under an indicator. In fact, he says, this can be good advice at any time of year.

The hexagenia hatch is the most exciting time to be on Fall River. These inch-and-a-half-long mayflies come to the surface just as dusk falls on the river. Trout that are normally cautious about taking anything abandon discretion and cruise just under the surface, gulping these giant insects late into the night.

Fishing the hex hatch is more of a social event, a happening, than good fishing. Fall River regulars admit that few fish are actually caught during this period, but the rising fish make it an incredible time to be on the river.

Anglers usually gather in the late afternoon to throw hex nymph or caddis pupa imitations. As evening approaches and the adult hexes begin popping to the surface, they switch to hex dries.

The hatch is so prolific that the chances of a trout taking your fly is pure luck. After nightfall, when it's too dark to see your hand much less untangle your back cast, the spinner fall occurs. Dead hexagenias form a thick mat on the river surface and the trout continue to cruise, gulping mouthfuls of the insects.

The hex hatch occurs on the lower river, from Tule River to the McArthur Road Bridge.

Access
The Dredge Site at Glenburn
From McArthur, take Glenburn Road 4.0 miles toward the Glenburn Church. The Department of Fish and Game has megotiated a lease for a launch area at the PG&E site.

Trailer boats are not allowed. Check with the Redding DFG or any of the tackle shops in the area for more specific information.

The Cal Trout Access
Take MacArthur Road 6.2 miles west from Fall River, turn right on Island Drive, drive 1.4 miles to the bridge. The access is just accross the bridge. Parking is very limited. The access is for boat launching only. Guides and boat rentals are unavailable.

The Fly Shop Outfitters/Rick's Lodge
Rick's Lodge and The Fly Shop access are located on Metzger Road on the upper river. Take MacArthur Road 8.6 miles west out of the town of MacArthur. River access, boat rentals and guides are available by prior arrangement from the Fly Shop Outfitters (916) 222-3555, or Rick's Lodge (916) 336-5300.

For More Information
Duane Milleman, The Fly Shop Outfitters, 4140 Churn Creek Road, Redding, CA 96002, (916) 243-5317.

PIT RIVER

Historically, the Pit River may well have been the finest trout stream in California, if not the West. One of the largest rivers in the state, it gets its name from the Pit Indians, a tribe that dug pits in the ground to trap game animals.

The river begins in the Warner Mountains near Alturas and flows southwest, winding its way through the high country of Modoc's Big Valley. Reservoirs and water diversions reduce the Pit to a slow, meandering stream as it crosses the valley floor. It skirts the Fall River Valley within whistling distance of the community of Fall River, then descends into a narrow, steep canyon carved from basalt and lava.

The character of the Pit River changes dramatically where it is joined by the Fall River as it roars out of the Pit No. 1 Powerhouse. Within the next few miles the stream is joined by Hat Creek at Lake Britton near the town of Burney.

Water from the McCloud River, piped through a tunnel from McCloud Reservoir to Iron Canyon Reservoir, is then released through the James Black Powerhouse into the Pit below the community of Big Bend. The Pit River ends in Shasta Lake, joining the Sacramento River as a source of the huge reservoir.

Each of these tributaries is a major stream in its own right, but by the time the Pit River enters Shasta Lake it has a minimum flow of 2,700 cubic feet per second (c.f.s.), making it the largest river in the state. The flows are made even more dramatic because power reservoirs feed each powerhouse. The flows are stored in the reservoirs when not needed, then released during the periods of peak power demands, usually during the day in the summer months.

The flow crossing the lowest dam on the pit, Pit Dam No. 7 just above the high water level of Shasta Lake, runs at 150 c.f.s. at night. But in minutes the flow will roar over

Brad Jackson

the dam at 8,000 c.f.s. when the Pit No. 7 Powerhouse turns on.

If rivers in the north of California were labeled by their major water sources, the Sacramento River below Shasta Dam would be named the Pit River and one of its tributaries would be a small stream called Sacramento Creek.

But consider the ramifications: The area from Redding south would be called the Pit River Valley and the state capital would probably still be in Vallejo because politicians would never move it to a town called Pitville.

Fishing Techniques

The Pit River is an enigma to anglers because it hasn't had the scrutiny that other streams have enjoyed. In the first place, very little of the Pit River is fishable since much of the stream bed in this area is buried under reservoirs. In other sections the current is much too strong for good fishing or, more important, for safety.

This leaves those few areas below each dam, where the bulk of the water is diverted from the river bed and piped several miles downstream to a powerhouse. Pacific Gas & Electric is obligated to maintain minimum flows of 150 c.f.s. on these stretches of the stream so that aquatic life, including insects and fish, can survive. These are the areas to fish.

Some of these areas are difficult to reach because access is very limited. Where there are roads, they do not follow within walking distance of the stream except for a couple of exceptions. One is the area below Lake Britton Dam to Powerhouse No. 3, the other is from Pit Dam No. 4 downstream to the Pit No. 4 Powerhouse. But the road follows the stream for only a short distance then it climbs above the canyon, leaving the river in a deep, narrow canyon.

The remaining stretches of fishable water are accessible only where the road crosses the river. Anglers must walk up or down stream along the stream bed.

Even from the stream, access is difficult. Boulders are large and hard to climb over. Wading is tough because of a slime that grows on rocks that are exposed, then covered as releases push the water level up and down.

As a result, knowledge about fishing the Pit River is general. Duane Milleman has fished it for several years and although he operates a guide service, The Fly Shop Outfitters in Redding, he is reluctant to take clients fishing on the Pit River.

The river is for the adventurous, for someone willing to walk in armed with very little knowledge about the fishery but with a very sturdy pair of boots. That someone must be also be very healthy.

Duane Milleman says, "The Pit River is not a classic dry fly fishery, most of the action is with nymphs.

"Fly fishing the Pit River requires only a knowledge of the patterns that aquatic insects follow," he says. "During the early season, stoneflies are very active," including the *Pteronarcys Californica*, the large salmon flies.

Large golden stones are also active early in the year. But don't bother with dry patterns unless you see fish taking adult stones off the surface, which usually occurs just before dusk. Fish nymphs instead—nymphs are in the river year round while the adults are active for only a short time.

"The patterns that I use are big and black," says Milleman, "and I get them down to the bottom."

Mayflies such as pale morning duns appear later in the season on the flat-water stretches. The water in the Pit is so dark that the pale morning duns are hard to spot, but Milleman says, "If you can see them, fish them."

The Pit also has some caddis. The hatches occur right at dusk. Use olive or tan Elk Hair Caddis when adults appear on the water, fish with caddis nymphs and emergers the rest of the time. If you see adult caddis on the surface but have no luck fishing with dries, switch to nymphs or emergers. These will catch fish even during the hatches.

Fishing slows down through the summer then picks up again in the fall. A big mayfly, a #8 isonychia, becomes active during the fall.

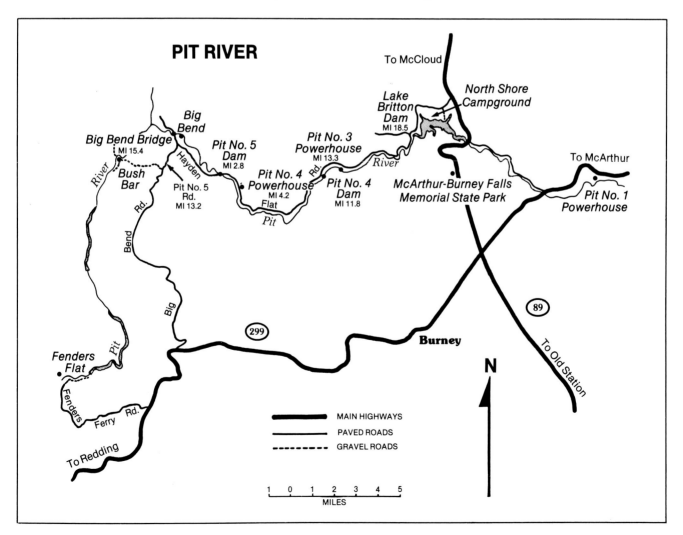

Because a large percentage of the fish in the Pit are cannibalistic, lure anglers can fish with Panther Martins, Little Cleos or Rebels and Rapalas. Bait anglers use night crawlers, grasshoppers or red eggs.

Access

Fender's Ferry

The turnoff to Fenders's Ferry Road is well marked, just 30.4 miles east on Highway 299 from the Interstate 5 turnoff. Turn left onto Fender's Ferry Road. The pavement ends at 3.5 miles. This road becomes fairly rough but not impassable for passenger cars.

Mile 8.4—Fenders Flat

The road forks. The right-hand fork is paved, follow it .3 of a mile to Forest Service Road 35N66. Four-tenths of a mile down a steep, bumpy road you will arrive at a flat, grassy field. This is Fenders Flat.

Corpulent rainbow prefer well oxygenated pocket water of the Pit. Weighted nymphs work best and sure footed wading of slippery substrate is a must. Brad Jackson

The road ends next to the dam. A sign warns people to stay off the dam because water levels may change without notice and sweep them from the top of the dam. Anglers can access the left side of the river by working their way along the cliffs below the dam. Access appears easier on the other side but there is no apparent way of getting there.

The reservoir behind the dam is surrounded with a chain link fence. It is easy to understand why PG&E wants to keep anglers and others away from the reservoir. The level of the reservoir and the current speed is directly influenced by the water going through Powerhouse No. 7 upstream. Even an alert angler could be caught in a sudden increase in the water release and swept over the dam.

When Shasta Lake is full the confluence is only a few hundred yards from the Dam. When the lake is low there may be several miles of stream to fish.

Because the water released from the dam is cold, fish from Shasta Lake congregate below the dam. In general, the water flows are so strong that fly fishing is difficult, but lures and bait work well in this area.

What is impressive is the water flow going over the dam. In the spring the flow equals that of the Klamath, the Deschutes or even the lower Sacramento.

The left-hand fork will take you to a high steel bridge that crosses the Pit River (Mile 8.7), then winds away up Potem Creek Canyon and loops around Shasta Lake. You can view Potem Creek Falls by stopping at the first wide area in the road. A quarter- mile trail leads to a viewing area of this spectacular waterfall.

Big Bend Road—Highway 299 to Big Bend

From Interstate 5, take the Highway 299 East exit from Redding. Do not get confused with the Highway 299 West Exit two miles to the south. You could find yourself going east on Highway 44 to Lassen Park, which may not fit your plans but will put you into some good fishing.

Continue east on highway 299 for 34.4 miles to the Hillcrest-Big Bend turnoff. Big Bend is 13 miles down a windy mountain road.

The intersection of Big Bend Road and Hagen Flat Road in the community of Big Bend is ground zero. Because the accesses to the Pit River are actually side roads off Big Bend Road we are using the intersection of Big Bend Road and Highway 299, just east of Round Mountain, as the starting point.

Mile 7.7—Road to Pit No. 6

This road is a blind alley and ends at a locked gate before it reaches the river.

Mile 13.2—Pit No. 5

A kiosk describes the recreation areas developed by PG&E. This road crosses the Pit River and continues to

Iron Canyon Reservoir where the McCloud River is held. Just 1.5 miles down the road it begins to descend sharply. There is a magnificent view of the Pit River Canyon, one of the steepest, most rugged canyons in California.

Mile 4.1—Pit No. 5

The road to Pit No. 5 Powerhouse crosses the Pit River. Here the river is a small freestone stream with large boulders. In some areas the river follows a single channel, in others it breaks up to form several small channels.

Continuing downstream leads to Pit No. 5 Powerhouse and James Black Powerhouse. A road next to the right side of the bridge leads down to the river and a large gravel bar. Fire rings mark old campsites. Although the road ends at the river, it is above the reservoir. There would be no way of returning from the reservoir to the road—the current is too strong and the river is too shallow for a powerboat.

The road ends at Pit No. 5 and the gorge is extremely narrow below there. Although it is part of the reservoir, it is no more than 50 feet wide and enclosed by sheer canyon walls.

A short distance above the bridge a road leads upstream to a paved area, the site of the old Brushy Bar School. Anglers can walk upstream or downstream from here but the going is tough. The boulders are large—two to three feet across, which means tough walking and difficult wading. It is necessary to ford the stream several times but the fishing can be worth it.

The river is open here and casting is fairly easy.

Mile 15.4—Big Bend Bridge

Big Bend Bridge crosses the river, which is fishable here and has the same large boulder character as at Pit No. 5. Nelson Creek Road winds up the left side of the river and a sign indicates that it ends 1.1 miles upriver.

The rainbow trout population in riffles and pools fed by now-mandatory releases from Lake Britton Dam has flourished due to enlightened bag and slot limits implemented by the California Department of Fish and Game. Brad Jackson

Fred Gordon fishing on the Upper Sacramento River. Bill Sunderland

Hagen Flat Road

Big Bend to Lake Britton
Hagen Flat Road intersects with Big Bend Road just inside the city limits of Big Bend. This intersection will be the starting point for the purposes of this book.

Mile 0.0
Hagen Flat Road and Big Bend Road.

Mile 2.8—Pit No. 5 Dam
A nice piece of freestone stream water extends below Pit No. 5 Dam for several hundred yards before entering the reservoir. Before crossing the dam, a dirt road to the right leads to Deep Camp Campground. From the campground it is possible to work upstream along the left-hand side (looking downstream) of the river.

The road crosses the bridge and continues upriver.

Mile 3.5
From here upstream to Powerhouse 4 the river flows very fast, too fast for good fishing or safety.

Mile 4.2—Pit No. 4 Powerhouse
It is possible to access the stream above the powerhouse, but there is no path. An angler will have to make his way through the riparian growth as best as he can.

The road follows the river about 100 feet above the stream, but it is a tough piece of water to get to. There is a true lack of accessibility to the Pit—anyone fishing above the Pit No. 4 Powerhouse is almost assured of not seeing another person on the stream.

But it can be done, and this is considered by Duane Milleman to be the best area of the Pit River to fish for trophy rainbows.

Mile 5.8
A sign warns anglers of sudden rises in the river channel and says those entering the canyon do so at their own risk. It is unlikely that anyone could make it to the river since the banks are very steep and heavily overgrown.

Mile 10.2
The road drops back to near river level. A side road leads down to an open gravel bar that runs along the river. The river is open and easy to get to at this point. It is fairly wide and uncluttered, offering good fly fishing and spin fishing.

Mile 10.7
Another road leads to the upper end of the gravel bar.

Mile 11.0
A road drops to a flat along the river. The river is easy to fish and one could camp here.

Mile 11.5
Another road leads to the river. A sign warns of sudden rises and cautions anglers to enter the stream at their own risk.

Mile 11.8—Pit Dam No. 4
The reservoir behind the dam is about one mile long. You may fish from the bank but boating and swimming are not allowed on the reservoir.

Mile 13.3—Pit No. 3 Powerhouse

Water from the powerhouse flows about half a mile until it reaches the reservoir behind Pit Dam No. 4. The water flow while the generator is running is much too high for fishing.

Mile 13.4
Below the Lake Britton Dam

When the Lake Britton Dam was built all the water was piped downstream several miles to the Pit No. 3 Powerhouse. Except for a few springs resulting from the hydraulic pressure in the aquifer created by Lake Britton, water no longer flowed in the river channel. The flow created by the springs was about 30 c.f.s. until Rock Creek entered the channel about one mile downstream. Although a small population of fish still inhabited the river, most of the fish and other aquatic life disappeared.

When the power license for Lake Britton came up for renewal in 1985, the Department of Fish and Game negotiated a minimum release of 150 c.f.s. through the old river channel. Gates were installed in the dam and in 1987 water flowed through this section of the Pit River for the first time in more than 60 years.

Now, the trout population in this part of the river has become a viable fishery. In fact, stream surveys indicate that the catch rate is higher than on lower Hat Creek, although this might be influenced by the numbers of anglers on Hat Creek and the difficulties in accessing this stretch of the Pit River.

In time, this may become the most celebrated stretch of water in California.

The character of the river is a typical pool and drop stream —the river drops quickly through rock piles then enters long, slow pools that appear to be good brown trout water. An angler can pick his or her water in this area.

There are fast-water sections where the current flows around and over large boulders. There are also slow pools where an angler can cast and retrieve small spoons and spinners, or crank bait lures such as Rapalas.

The fly angler can fish mayflies in their various forms, but nymph fishing is the best all-around bet.

Be careful, wading is not easy.

Mile 16.2

The road climbs above the river, but once an angler hikes into the canyon walking along the river is reasonably easy. The stream is good, fishable water and there are open areas to fish from the gravel bars.

Mile 18.5
Lake Britton Dam

Mile 19.2

The turnoff to the dam. A kiosk advises anglers of the recreational opportunities that PG&E provides.

Mile 21.9—North Shore Campground

This is a PG&E public campground. There is no drinking water but it offers access to Lake Britton for swimming and fishing.

Mile 22.8

Hagen Flat Road, now known as Clark Creek Road, intersects with Highway 89.

Highway 89
Clark Creek Road to Highway 299

Highway 89 passes the accesses to Lake Britton and the entrance to McArthur-Burney Falls State Park.

Mile 0.0
Highway 89 and Clark Creek Road

Mile 2.1
Lake Britton Fishing Access.

This is an improved boat ramp and parking area.

Lake Britton is best noted for its crappie fishing. It has black bass, but it's a tough lake to fish. Other species include bluegill and catfish. The trout population is a cool weather fishery that is best during the winter and early spring. During the late summer heavy algae blooms dominate the lake, making it unpleasant to fish or water ski.

Mile 2.4
Lake Britton Highway Bridge.

A road to the left on the north end of the bridge leads to Dusty Campground and follows the lake to its upper end.

Mile 4.2
McArthur-Burney Falls State Park

This is a full-service California state campground with campsites, gift shop, store and fast food stand.

Mile 10.9
Intersection of Highway 89 and Highway 299

The Outpost Restaurant and bar is located on this corner. Turn left to reach the upper Pit River. Turn right to go to the town of Burney and to return to Redding.

Highway 299
The Upper Pit River
Pit No. 1 Powerhouse

Turn left from Highway 89 onto Highway 299, drive north past Hat Creek, over the Pit River Bridge and on up the hill. A sign on the right marks the road to Pit No. 1 Powerhouse. A recreation area for PG&E employees is on the left. To the right is a large flat area with unimproved camping areas.

This is an access for anglers and for white water recreation. This area of the Pit River does have good-sized trout but its flows are very erratic. The stream is heavily lined with willows and the stream bottom is slimy and very tough to wade.

For More Information

Duane Milleman, Fly Shop Outfitters, 4140 Churn Creek Rd., Redding, CA 96002.

Chapter Eleven

TRUCKEE RIVER

All summer long Californians pour along Interstate 80 to Lake Tahoe and Reno to gamble, gambol and enjoy some of the most beautiful scenery in the state. Considering the popularity of the area and the easy access, there is surprisingly little fishing pressure on the Truckee River.

It is doubly surprising since it harbors large fish, notably wild browns, in addition to the smaller rainbows that are stocked in some areas.

Perhaps the answer is that the Truckee River is not that easy to fish. The best parts are big, broad and move quickly through rapids and runs. It can be excellent for fly fishing, but aggressive wading is necessary.

There also is a 12-mile stretch of the river that is designated as a wild trout section, with artificial lures, barbless hooks and a limit on both catch and size. The section begins at the city of Truckee and runs to Boca Bridge. Since it is ideal for fly fishing it often gets more pressure than the rest of the river.

The flow of the Truckee from Lake Tahoe is controlled by a dam in Tahoe City. Although the river is closed to fishing for its first 1,000 feet, it is always fun to spend a few minutes on the bridge over the river just below the small dam and watch five-pound rainbows feeding.

They have the assurance of fish that know there is no danger from above as they concentrate on making the most of the constant supply of food washed into the headwaters from Lake Tahoe.

The first section of the Truckee River, which runs 4.2 miles to River Ranch at the turnoff to Alpine Meadows ski resort, is mostly deep pools and fairly slow water better suited to bait and lure fishing than to flies. From River Ranch to the city of Truckee, the river is mostly riffles with a few runs and is easily accessible from Highway 89 for almost its entire length.

This 14-mile stretch of water from Tahoe City to the

Ralph Cutter

confluence of Donner Creek as the river enters Truckee doesn't qualify as a blue ribbon trout stream. However, it is a great area for family fishing. There are campgrounds along the river and many more areas where a car can be parked a few steps from the water. There even is a paved bike path upstream from River Ranch.

This is a stocked section of the river and the planted rainbows can be taken on lures, bait or flies. Much of the water is open enough to allow easy casting for fly anglers and most of the year it is low enough for wading, although the stone bottom of the stream can be tough going and a wading staff is handy to have.

There are a few wild trout, mostly browns in the eight to 10 inch range.

This is a popular rafting area when the water is high and while it is big enough to accommodate both anglers and rafters it's a good idea to keep an eye out while wading.

Randy Johnson of Johnson Tackle and Guide Service in Tahoma guides in the Truckee and Tahoe area.

"The thing about the Truckee is that you need a high expertise level to be successful. Tactics on the Truckee are not different than on the Upper Sacramento or McCloud Rivers," Johnson says.

For the 14-mile section from Tahoe City to the city of Truckee, Johnson says that during the early season there are baetis hatches, some midges and a small Western green drake. Since temperatures at that elevation are cold, nymphs are important for the fly angler.

"One of the dynamite nymphs is the Gold Ribbed Hare's Ear," he notes. "In addition, I tie a marabou AP series which is a fantastic fly for me. It is in black, brown, olive and green and is weighted, usually tied in about a #10 through #16."

In riffles and runs Johnson also suggests using caddis and little yellow stone nymphs. Caddis are good from June through

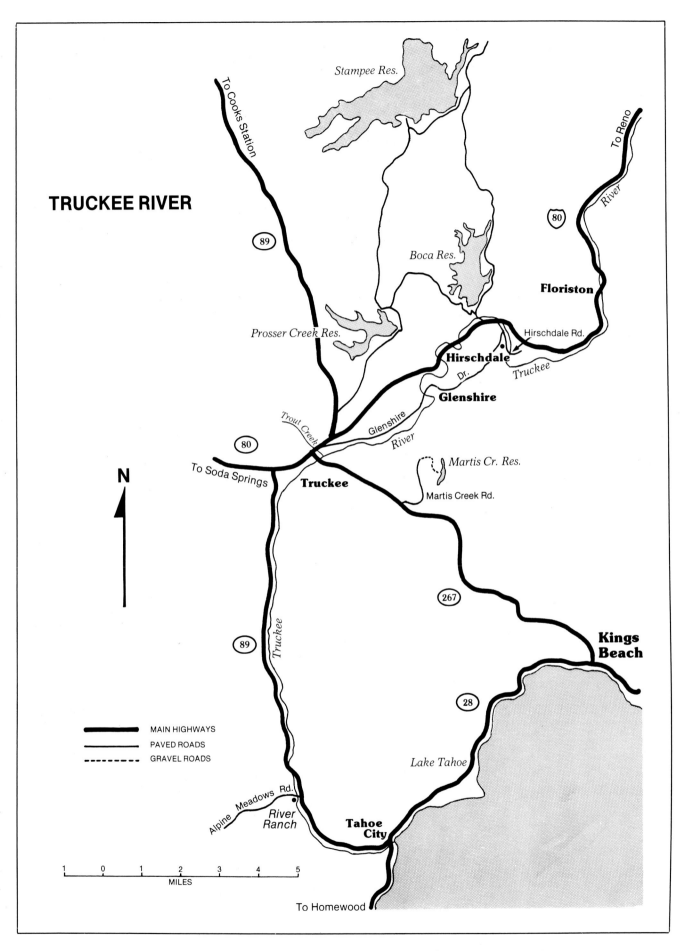

TRUCKEE RIVER

Stampee Res.

To Cooks Station

To Reno

89

80

River

Boca Res.

Floriston

Prosser Creek Res.

Hirschdale Rd.

Hirschdale

Dr.

Truckee

Glenshire

Trout Creek

Glenshire

River

80

Martis Cr. Res.

To Soda Springs

Truckee

Martis Creek Rd.

N

267

Kings Beach

89

Truckee

28

Lake Tahoe

MAIN HIGHWAYS

PAVED ROADS

GRAVEL ROADS

Alpine Meadows Rd.

River Ranch

Tahoe City

1 0 1 2 3 4 5
MILES

To Homewood

the rest of the summer.

For hardware anglers, Z-Rays in the quarter ounce size, Rooster Tails, Panther Martins in yellow with red dots or black with yellow dots, are effective. Johnson says that "one lure that is effective is a Rapala CD11 to CD7 in gold and silver. Some of the locals who are religious about Rapalas take some big fish out of there with these."

When fall arrives, there is good baetis fishing along with stonefly nymphs.

As the river passes through the city of Truckee, from Donner Creek to Trout Creek just east of town, is not worth fishing. Trout Creek, which enters the river on the eastern edge of Truckee where the old logging mill is located, is where the wild trout section starts.

To get to the wild trout section, take Highway 267 from Truckee toward Interstate 80. Turn to the right on Glenshire Drive just outside town. Glenshire Drive passes above the old logging mill, where the wild trout section begins at Trout Creek, and then parallels the river for the next four miles.

The Southern Pacific Railroad tracks run between the road and the river, but there are numerous parking areas alongside the tracks. An easy walk of only a few hundred yards through the sagebrush takes anglers to the Truckee.

Evening fishing is often very productive. Ralph Cutter

Since most of the land belongs to the Department of Fish and Game, there is no private property to cut off access.

The first section of the wild trout water just outside Truckee is meandering and is easier water to fish than the lower, fast-water area. Fishing isn't as good there as some other areas, although there are some good pockets. Part of the problem is that the water in this area warms up more in low-flow drought years. It also is the area most heavily fished by fly anglers.

"This is a very easy area for the novice to learn to fish," Johnson says. "It is a good dry fly area, with good mayfly hatches most of the season and very good nymphing in the larger holes. You can also classify it as some of the best streamer water in the river—I took a 10 pound, 6 ounce brown there."

This area extends about four miles to where Glenshire Drive crosses the old Highway 40 Bridge just west of Glenshire. Upstream from the bridge is a favorite area to fish. But downstream is a three-mile stretch of the river that belongs to the San Francisco Flycasters and is closed to public fishing.

The private section is well-posted. Rulings by California courts have made it possible for anglers to wade rivers and fish, so long as they do not step onto private land, but since the river is difficult to wade and the private section is patrolled, trying to fish it would be more trouble than it is worth.

After crossing the bridge, Glenshire Drive moves away from the Truckee so there is no easy access—even if somebody wanted to trespass. The private section ends at the Union Hill causeway.

Four miles beyond the bridge, Glenshire Drive intersects with Hirschdale Road, which goes to the Boca Bridge area. Glenshire Drive dead-ends at an auto wrecking yard after three miles, but from where it crosses the river along an old steel bridge to the yard is good fishing. The access is not as easy as in the Truckee area—a short hike into the canyon is necessary—but nymphing is excellent. There also are whitefish in this section.

Johnson says "it's a lot of water, this is where the river is the biggest. There is limited wading and an angler needs to be careful. It is mostly hard, rock bottom, a freestone stream with a high PH factor.

"This is a good area because of the limited access, it takes a little hoofing. It's big fly area—use good-sized streamers, Zonkers and big stonefly nymphs sized #4 and #6."

Following Hirschdale Road instead of Glenshire Drive at the intersection leads to I-80 and Boca Bridge, where the wild trout section ends.

The Boca Bridge section is an excellent area to fish.

"Upstream nymphing is the way to go and can produce 25-fish days," Johnson says. "Use short-line tactics, which offer good control. About all these areas are wadable since you can get around the larger holes."

He suggests that anglers work their way into position to cast to the prime feeding lies.

"During the early and late season there also is fantastic dry fly activity, with caddis and little yellow stones during the summer months. There are at least 10 different mayflies on the Truckee, along with three types of caddis—microcaddis, green caddis and spotted caddis."

Johnson says flies imitating speckled dace and Lahontan redside shiners, common throughout the area, are very effective.

"Big browns really go for these," he says, noting that the Truckee is open to night fishing and most of the trophy brown trout are taken then.

Anglers who wish to stay on the wild trout section of the Truckee can backtrack by using the access to I-80 at Boca Bridge. Just follow I-80 West toward Truckee as it criss-crosses the river and take advantage of any of the several turnoffs that allow roadside parking. Don't park on the highway since it is heavily patrolled and you're sure to pick up a ticket.

Downstream from Boca Bridge is another 10 miles of the Truckee River, ending at Gray Creek, that is restricted to a two trout limit. In the Hirschdale area there are some deep pools that are excellent for bait fishermen. Johnson says he has snorkled the pools "and there are some big trout in there. All the holes have at least a couple of five-pounders."

Rapalas are effective, Johnson says, adding that there also are some good areas for fly fishermen, who on cloudy days do very well with midges.

The three-mile stretch of deep water from Hirschdale to Floriston flattens out as it goes into the Floriston area. Although the dirt road along the river at the Floriston exit of I-80 is blocked off, it is possible to use it to walk to the river.

The Truckee is strictly a fast-water river the rest of the way to the Nevada border, following I-80 all the way. Just make sure to park off I-80—there are plenty of places—since it is easy to get a ticket from the California Highway Patrol.

From Floriston downstream a flume takes some of the water out of the river for several miles. The trout are still there but the water can be low enough to make fishing difficult.

Martis Lake

One of the most famous fly fishing lakes in California, Martis is what Randy Johnson describes as "a classroom for stillwater fishing."

Strictly a catch-and-release, barbless artificial lure area, Martis is a great float tube and pram lake.

"It has freshwater shrimp, callibaetis, little yellow sallies at the creek mouths and a premier hatch of blood midges. Overall, there is a good insect structure, although there have been some problems caused by the fertilization of the golf course at Northstar."

The road to Martis is three miles southeast of the town of Truckee on Highway 267 towards Kings Beach. The "Martis Creek Reservoir" turnoff to the left is clearly marked and the paved road leads two miles to a campground that is just above the reservoir.

Easily accessible, Martis is the home of big browns and rainbows. It's one of those lakes where knowledge is power since the right fly at the right time is an absolute necessity to be successful.

Johnson uses Martis both for classes and for clients when guiding.

"Browns can be hunted with blood midges and callibaetis," he says. "There also are small chironomid hatches in the evening. In the summer try blood midges from early to mid-morning, either as emergers or adults. It is strictly long-leader nymphing, with 16- to 25-foot leaders. There also are a lot of springs in the lake, so in mid-summer look for spring activity and fish those areas.

"From the opening of fishing season for about the first month, use Woolly Buggers and attractors. Then callibaetis, parachute callibaetis and other standard patterns, including Parachute Hare's Ears and Parachute Adams."

Johnson recommends 4 weight rods and light tippets, either #6 or #7.

Ralph Cutter with a beautiful Truckee rainbow. Ralph Cutter

Boca, Stampede And Prosser Reservoirs

All three reservoirs are accessible from I-80—Prosser from Highway 89 leading north from Truckee, and Boca and Stampede from the Boca exit of I-80.

"They can be fantastic during ice out," Randy Johnson says. "When the ice begins to break up in the spring, from mid-March to mid-April, it's great to fish shallow water with nymphs, streamers and Woolly Buggers. Use sinking line tactics."

For bait fishermen, Power Bait is effective.

For More Information

Randy Johnson, Johnson Tackle and Guide Service, P.O. Box 26, Tahoma, CA 95733, (916) 525-6575.

Chapter Twelve

NORTH FORK STANISLAUS RIVER

The north fork of the Stanislaus River, stretching 65 miles from its headwaters near Lake Alpine in the Sierra Nevada to the placid reservoir backed up behind the New Melones Dam, is the centerpiece of one of California's least known and most under-utilized fishing areas. Only three hours from the San Francisco Bay Area, the Stanislaus and the mountain streams that feed it are teeming with trout.

There are high mountain lakes and tumbling creeks. The river itself grows from a brook-sized trickle to a swift-moving river of rapids and deep pools. It finally ends in the 23-mile-long expanse of the New Melones Reservoir, completed in 1979 after a decade-long battle between the government and environmentalists.

And all this in some of the most spectacular mountain scenery California has to offer.

Outside the New Melones Reservoir, trophy-sized trout are rare in the Stanislaus ecosystem. But the number and variety of fish make up for it. Browns, brookies and rainbows abound and almost every stream or lake offers fishing possibilities.

There are a limited number of easy-access points to the Stanislaus and some of its more popular feeder streams, with paved roads, campgrounds and a constant supply of rainbows stocked by the California Department of Fish and Game. These areas tend to be the center of the put-and-take, family-style fishing. But half a mile upstream or downstream an angler often can find both wild trout and solitude. And even the easy-access areas, with some exceptions, are not crowded during weekdays.

Since the north fork of the Stanislaus runs deep in a canyon for its entire length, getting to private fishing isn't a stroll across a grassy meadow. During the spring melt in high-water years the river comes smashing through the canyon, leaving a tangle of down timber, boulders and rocks that make

Bill Sunderland

slow going for the angler searching for likely holes. On the other hand, that same jumble of rocks and timber offers the type of cover and variety of water that guarantees fish in just about any section of the river where you drop a line.

Fly fishing and bait fishing are excellent for almost the entire length of the Stanislaus, while spin-fishing varies according to the area. For bait anglers, the usual smorgasbord of worms, salmon eggs, crickets and artificial baits all work well. The steady supply of planters—the DFG regularly stocks rainbows in a number of areas during the spring/summer season—will take about anything when they are on the bite. The natives, including good-sized browns lurking in deep holes, are more selective. Many local anglers prefer crickets during most of the season, although Power Bait is coming on fast.

Zeroing in on the proper patterns for fly fishing the north fork of the Stanislaus is a tougher proposition, particularly since the character of the river changes, as does its entomology, as it drops from almost 7,500 feet to 1,000 feet at New Melones Reservoir. The variety of stoneflies, caddis and mayflies changes along the way, but there is always a plentiful supply of food for trout.

Hatches are neither as prolific nor as regular as on more placid streams. The lack of fly fishing activity on the Stanislaus has one negative—it means there is no reliable information that provides dates and types of fly hatches that are valuable in choosing patterns to tie and use. As a result, attractors such as Humpies and Royal Wulffs are the general rule. Other effective dries include Elk Hair Caddis and Black Ants, both with and without wings.

For nymphs, Zug Bugs, PTs, Hare's Ears and Casual Dress are always popular. Where knowledgeable local anglers have specific suggestions for certain areas, they are included. But any fly fisherman would do well to check what is in the

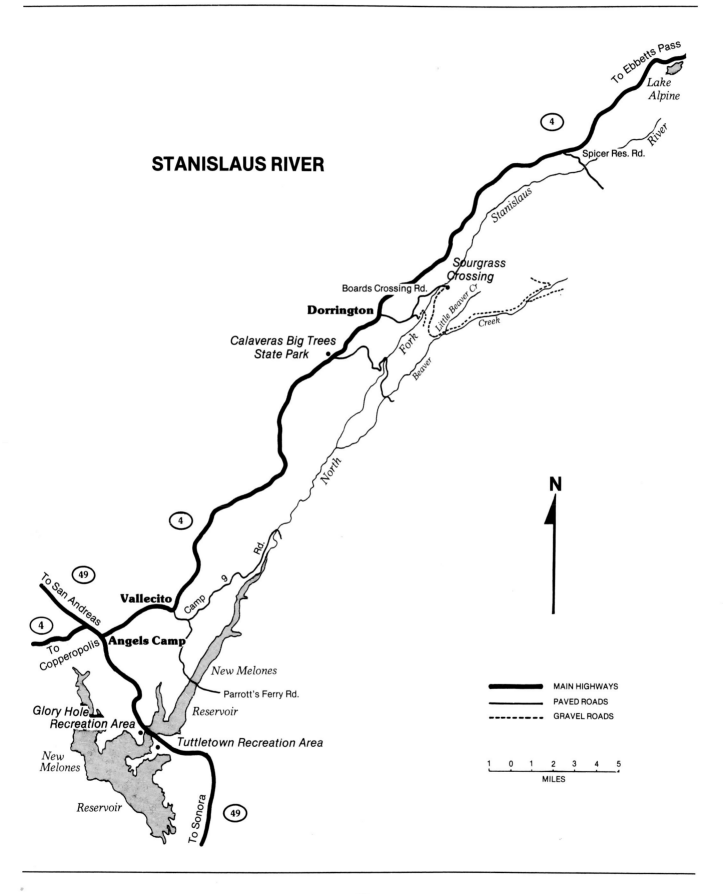

STANISLAUS RIVER

To Ebbetts Pass

Lake Alpine

④

River

Stanislaus

Spicer Res. Rd.

Spurgrass Crossing

Boards Crossing Rd.

Dorrington

Little Beaver Cr

Beaver

Creek

Calaveras Big Trees State Park

Fork

North

Rd.

Camp 9

④

Vallecito

⑭

To San Andreas

④

To Copperopolis

Angels Camp

New Melones

Parrott's Ferry Rd.

Reservoir

Glory Hole Recreation Area

New Melones

Reservoir

Tuttletown Recreation Area

To Sonora

⑭

N

▬▬▬▬	MAIN HIGHWAYS
——	PAVED ROADS
- - - - -	GRAVEL ROADS

1 0 1 2 3 4 5

MILES

gravel and on the rocks of the area being fished and to take time to identify any hatch that may come off the water.

There are no fly-fishing-only or catch-and-release areas along the north fork of the Stanislaus at this time and this is not likely to change in the foreseeable future.

Peter and Nicole Cooper, who own Creekside Sporting Goods on Highway 4 in Murphys, have fished the Stanislaus for years and both are guides for the area. Peter notes that "there are very few spots where you can get in and cast. You've got to work for it. Most people want to drive to the fishing spot and get out and lean against the car. They want to pull into a parking lot and go right there."

Nicole says that for most of the Stanislaus, the same patterns have shown themselves reliable, with not that much change as the river broadens and works its way down to New Melones.

She recommends Hare's Ears, Zug Bugs, Peeking Caddis and some other caddis patterns, including the Sundance Special and Elk Hair Caddis.

"These are good standards early in the season," she says. "Work them just under the film or floated high. The average size is going to be a 14. You don't need 18 and 20, and a lot of people use 12 and even 10.

"It depends on your outlook. A lot of people think the bigger the hook the bigger the fish, which is something we kind of go with."

As the season progresses, Nicolle Cooper says that "grasshoppers are popular, along with ants. Early in the summer, use green grasshoppers and later on try brown."

Highway 4 is the main access route to the north fork of the Stanislaus and is never more than a few miles away from the canyon all the way from Angels Camp to Lake Alpine. However, access to the river at the canyon bottom is limited, with only a few entry points along its entire length.

The character of the river may change in coming years with the construction of the new Spicer Reservoir. The reservoir, completed in 1988 and replacing a smaller lake, will do much to moderate the flow of the river year around, but at the same time it means the spring runoff that flushed the river won't be nearly as strong and as a result heavier silting is expected.

New Melones Reservoir

The creation of the New Melones Reservoir destroyed one of the most popular white water sections of the Stanislaus and caused a bitter battle with conservationists, a fight so heated that one protester chained himself to a river-side rock, threatening to allow himself to be drowned as the water level rose to fill the lake.

The protest was briefly effective and the reservoir was not filled to capacity. However, in the long run the government won and a stretch of river that attracted 50,000 rafters and kayakers annually disappeared under the placid surface of the reservoir. New Melones was dedicated and filling began from the north, middle and south forks of the Stanislaus in 1979, 35 years after the original authorization in 1944 to build the dam.

Calaveras Big Trees State Park. William J. Raymond

Although the legal battles continued, including fights over whether it could be filled to its limit, New Melones was from then on a fact, although it took until 1983 to fill to capacity for the first time. At capacity, it is capable of holding 2.4 million acre feet of water, with 20 square miles of surface. Its shoreline when full is almost 100 miles.

While white water enthusiasts still lament the loss of a prime run on the north fork of the Stanislaus, New Melones Reservoir has developed into an excellent fishery.

Easily accessible from the Bay Area and such Central Valley cities as Stockton, Merced and Fresno, New Melones is a major water playground. On summer weekends it is a haven for water skiers and power boaters, along with houseboats that are kept on the lake or which can be rented at the lakeside marina.

But there is enough space on the 23-mile-long lake for anglers to fish without worrying about being run over by speeding powerboaters or waterskiers. And there are plenty of nooks and coves that are out of the way.

Bank fishing is limited because few roads go to the water, so fishing from boats is almost a necessity. There are rainbow, German brown and Eagle Lake trout, including some trophy-sized monsters, along with largemouth bass, catfish, crappie and bluegill. Unlike most streams and rivers, it is legal to fish 24 hours a day and there is no season—you can fish year 'round.

Facilities And Access

The U.S. Bureau of Reclamation, which runs New Melones, has developed two recreation areas, the Glory Hole Recreation Area and Tuttletown Recreation Area. Both are off Highway 49 between Angels Camp and Sonora. Glory Hole is on the Angels Camp side of the lake and Tuttletown on the Sonora side. Highway 49 crosses New Melones at Stevenot Bridge.

The two recreation areas have nearly 300 campsites available, along with boat launch ramps. Glory Hole also offers permanent restrooms with hot and cold water and a sewage dump station. There is no fee for day use of the recreation areas or boat ramps, but there is a fee for overnight camping. There are no camping reservations—first come, first served.

The camping areas are well away from the water, particularly when the lake is below its peak elevation level of 1,088 feet, and no camping is allowed outside the designated areas or on the shore. Glory Hole, a privately-owned marina, has boat and houseboat rentals, gasoline, food and mooring.

There also is access but few facilities at Parrott's Ferry Bridge, which can be reached by taking Parrott's Ferry Road from Vallecito, four miles east of Angels Camp on Highway 4. Turning off to the left of Parrott's Ferry road about a mile from Vallecito is Camp Nine Road, which crosses the long arm of New Melones Lake where the north fork of the Stanislaus enters the reservoir at Camp Nine Bridge.

When the reservoir is full, Camp Nine Bridge is where the reservoir is generally considered to start and is the favorite area for a number of local trout anglers.

Fishing

Trolling with lures is the best year-around bet. But where the fish are found can vary, depending on the water temperature. Be advised, there are numerous 10-pounders waiting to be caught, so don't undersize your tackle.

For the lunkers, winter is best, with trolling on the surface using minnow imitations such as Rapalas, Rebels and Broken Backs. In the late spring, the trout start to go deeper, and larger lures trolled on lead core at up to 30 feet are effective.

Tom Schachten, who owns Glory Hole Sports on Highway 49 near Angels Camp, has lived in the area all his life and has fished New Melones since it was built. He advises that like most such big bodies of water, "Fishing in New Melones goes in cycles, and as you come to different times of the year then you use different things."

Pocket water on the North Fork of the Stanislaus River just downstream from Sourgrass Crossing holds numerous rainbows but most of them are planters. Bill Sunderland

The key, he says, is knowing where the thermocline is —that layer of water between the warm surface water and the colder deep water where fish are the most comfortable. Generally speaking, as the summer wears on and the sun heats the water, the thermocline gets deeper and deeper, and fewer and fewer fish can be found near the surface.

The other key factor at New Melones is threadfin shad, which provide an abundance of food for larger trout, particularly browns. Unless it is an unusual year, the fish start moving to the surface in November. The best fishing for rainbows comes along about Thanksgiving and extends through December, Schachten says.

"That's when the shore fishing starts. An angler can see shad jumping on the surface and can go to some of the points and coves where the trout come in very close and use nightcrawlers and Power Bait." Another suggestion is to fish for a couple of hours before daylight using a lighted bobber.

Most of the trout, Schachten says, are rainbows weighing three pounds and more. The lake is heavily planted by the DFG and because of the abundance of shad, a rainbow that was a pound when planted in June can be up to three pounds by fall and four pounds by the following spring.

"Most of the native fish that ran up and down the river are gone, and the planters don't know to go upriver, so they come in to shore."

The inshore fishing for rainbows lasts until February, when they move to deeper water where they can be taken by trolling. In spring, the thermocline begins and slowly moves down as the heat progresses, finally getting to 80 or 90 feet by late summer, making deep trolling the only way to get fish.

Fall colors on the Stanislaus. Brad Jackson

Browns are more difficult to catch, Schachten says. "The only time you get German browns is in late March, April, May and part of June, when they live along the shoreline, just like a bass. On some lakes you can catch browns on flies under the right conditions, but on Melones you really won't have much luck with flies."

With rainbows, he says, the best bet for flies is "around the beginning of February, if there are hatches. You also can get some on the surface in the morning by using a shad pattern when they are out chasing shad."

He says a fly imitating shad "is basically the same as spinfishing with Krokodiles or Kastmasters."

The biggest brown pulled out of New Melones so far has been more than 16 pounds, but it probably was a wild trout there before the dam was built, Schachten says. Most of the

German browns in the lake came from an unplanned plant by the DFG in 1984 when a truck carrying thousands of small browns broke down and the fish were dumped into New Melones rather than allowed to die. It is that group of fish that are now in the seven pound range, although they are becoming fewer and fewer each year since they have not spawned. Schachten says the DFG is planning to plant more browns since the first accidental plant was so successful.

Stanislaus River Calaveras Big Trees State Park

The most popular area to fish, Calaveras Big Trees State Park, is three miles east of Arnold on Highway 4. A paved road makes its way the six miles from the park entrance ($3 per car entrance fee) to the Stanislaus.

At the bridge crossing the river the DFG stocks heavily, and with good reason since it is a put-and-take fishing area popular with families. For a nice weekend with the kids, this is probably the best area on the river. A 75-site campground with first-rate facilities is just inside the entrance to the park, and the setting among the huge trees is lovely. There is a second campground with almost as many sites about half-way to the river, but no camping is allowed on the Stanislaus.

For a dedicated fly fisherman...well, it might be better to go to one of the less-used parts of the river.

Sourgrass Crossing

Another popular spot on the river, Sourgrass Crossing, is reached by following Board's Crossing Road from Dorrington, three miles east of Calaveras Big Trees on Highway 4. The paved, two-lane road winds its way down into the canyon, where a single-lane bridge crosses the river.

Just over the bridge there is a campground with toilets and drinking water. There aren't many campsites and it is generally crowded on weekends and rarely empty even on weekdays. The river here is stocked with rainbows. Fishing bait near the bridge, particularly upstream, is generally productive, but pressure is so heavy during the entire season that native fish are almost non-existent.

A dirt road at the upper end of the campground parallels the river for about half a mile upstream and some four-wheel enthusiasts are willing to risk their shock absorbers to ease their way over the rocks, but it is tough going. At the end of the road are several undeveloped areas that make nice camping, however, and it is a good area to use as a jumping-off point to work upstream.

Fishing upstream can be excellent. Every few hundred yards farther along the river means that much less possibility of sharing the river with others. It also means getting away from stocked trout and looking for more wily natives, including browns that run 14 inches or better. As usual, the browns tend to inhabit deeper water and nymphs are about the only way to get them to take. Rainbows generally are not big—most in the nine or 10-inch range—but they'll respond to a dry fly, particularly in the pocket water that makes up a good portion of the river. Working along the bank is not easy, which is one reason the fishing traffic dwindles quickly. There are few

Four to five pound rainbows are not uncommon. Brad Jackson

places where the Stanislaus is shallow enough to be waded easily until late in the season.

It is typical Sierra country, heavily wooded with large fir and pine trees. Black-tail deer are common in the area, but so are rattlesnakes, so keep your eyes open for both.

Fishing downstream from Sourgrass Crossing is easier going. Although the angler can follow the river, the first few hundred yards are unfishable rapids. It's easier to drive another quarter of a mile along the road after it crosses the bridge, park any place you can find enough room off the road, and then work your way down to the river. Several paths lead to the river and a five-minute walk will get you there. In addition to small falls and good pocket water, there also are some deep holes that the larger trout call home. But moving these big trout with bait or nymphs is difficult—they've been fished over for years and have learned their lessons well.

A trail follows the river so hiking is not as difficult as it is upstream. The river can be crossed during the late season when it is down, but fishing from the bank or from rocks in the river allows the angler to cover just about every stretch of water. Fly fishermen with reasonably proficient casting skills should have no problems at all.

Caddis and stoneflies are the main fare but heavy hatches are rare. Attractors, size #12 or #14, are the best all-around producers for dry fly fishermen. For browns, size #10 or #12 Casual Dress Nymphs can occasionally find a taker.

From Sourgrass an angler can fish all the way to Board's Crossing, about a mile downstream. Or Board's Crossing can be reached by a dirt road that leaves Board's Crossing Road

(the paved road known as Board's Crossing Road actually goes to Sourgrass crossing) just as it begins to work its way down into the canyon from Dorrington. It isn't clearly marked, but is the only other road going to the river. Although the four-mile drive down is steep on the one-lane road, four-wheel drive is not necessary.

At the river are several houses and access to the Stanislaus is limited on either side of the bridge. However, an eighth of a mile after crossing the river there is a campground that allows easy access and is not as crowded as the one at Sourgrass Crossing.

Beaver Creek

From both Calaveras Big Trees State Park and Sourgrass Crossing there is access to a Stanislaus tributary that can provide good early-season fishing, particularly for fly anglers who want action when the season opens and the Stanislaus is too high and fast for flies.

At Big Trees Park the paved road continues for another three and a half miles after crossing the Stanislaus before it reaches Beaver Creek. There is a picnic area, but no overnight camping is allowed. California DFG stocks rainbows here and at several other nearby spots on the creek. It's a great place for family fishing. Catching planters is almost guaranteed, a key ingredient for maintaining fishing interest with the youngsters. Trails follow the creek for some way so working upstream or downstream also is easy in this area.

To get to Beaver Creek by way of Sourgrass Crossing,

71

continue along Board's Crossing Road up the side of the canyon after crossing the river. At the top of the canyon, the paved road ends and the dirt road that begins there splits. To the left is the road to Rattlesnake Creek, which has some nice camping spots but offers only mediocre fishing. It also makes a complete loop of about 15 miles to join the Beaver Creek road.

Following the right fork for five miles leads to Beaver Creek. It is a heavily-logged area belonging to the Louisiana Pacific lumber company, which keeps it open for fishing in the summer. A gate one mile along the dirt road is locked in the off-season to prevent visitors from taking firewood out of the forest.

At Beaver Creek the road once again splits. The right fork crosses the creek and continues another 40 rugged miles to Beardsley Reservoir. The left branch parallels Beaver Creek for another five miles, allowing access at just about any point. Only a hundred yards down the road there is a pretty meadow campground set up by Louisiana Pacific with flat campsites and toilets.

Calaveras Big Trees State Park. William J. Raymond

Otherwise, campers can pick just about any open spot along the creek—there are plenty of them. Campfire permits generally are not required, but during exceptionally dry years the rules may change, including closing the area to all visitors.

The first mile or so of Beaver Creek after the road forks is the most popular area and is stocked with rainbows. Continuing upstream leads to a more defined canyon, with riffles and pocket water where small trout abound. In the spring and early summer they are eager and will readily take just about any fly offered. Size #14 or #16 Black Flying Ants almost always are a winner.

Five miles upstream, shortly after crossing a small bridge where Little Beaver Creek joins the main creek, the road forks again at a large meadow along the stream—perfect for camping. But best do it early in the season since most years cattle are brought into the area for summer grazing and once they arrive it is like camping or fishing in a stockyard.

Once past the meadow, the right fork of the road moves away from the creek, while after half a mile the left fork also begins to climb and easy access is lost. The left fork follows the ridge line to make a 15-mile loop and becomes the Rattlesnake Creek Road going back to the paved Sourgrass Crossing Road.

There are a lot of rainbows in Beaver Creek, feeding on caddis, stoneflies and mayflies, but most are small, in the six- to ten-inch range. There also are small brookies. Like the Stanislaus River, an angler can work along the creek far enough to guarantee private fishing, but there is enough stream-side brush so the going occasionally can be tough.

The stream, even when the spring runoff is underway, is always small enough to wade with ease. The Sierra setting is lovely and unless you're looking for trophy trout it is a fun place to fish.

Spicer Reservoir Road

This is the last paved-road access to the north fork and has some of the best fishing. In addition, the Stanislaus is smaller at this level—5,900 feet—and can be waded by more aggressive anglers. The campground at the river, four miles from Highway 4, has toilets, water and several dozen campsites set among the tall pines.

But the game is the same—fish for planters within a few hundred yards of the crossing or make your way along the Stanislaus until you are as far from other anglers as suits your fancy. Downstream there are some deep pools, but it takes more than an hour's hiking to get to the first of them. And be prepared to wade. Once away from the campground, the best way of getting downstream is to cross from one side of the river to the other as the terrain demands.

Lake Alpine

This spectacular High Sierra lake set at 7,350 feet alongside Highway 4 has become increasingly popular each year. With numerous lakeside campgrounds, a store and restaurant, it's an ideal outdoor retreat. And the trout fishing can be excellent.

While a boat or float tube is best, angling from bankside can be very productive, particularly off the rocky point jutting into the lake on the highway side or near the dam at the western end of Alpine. Bait or lures work best, particularly in the summer when an angler must go deep to find where the fish are holding.

For lures, Nicole Cooper of Creekside Sports in Murphys recommends "trolling from a boat with little flatfish, silver and greens. I recommend that people start close to the surface and work down until they find where the fish are. Early in the season—May, June and into July—the water still is pretty cold. The later you get, the deeper you want to go."

If you are stuck bankside, she says that "you can go any place you have water. Use spinners or spoons, or you can work a flatfish. Work the coves with them or go to the rocks by the dam."

For flies, the same patterns that are effective on the Stanislaus are the best when the fish are working topside. Late evening hatches occasionally have been known to excite the trout so much that the water looks like it is boiling in some places. Lucky is the angler with a boat or float tube close enough to work such a hatch.

The problem comes when the trout are holding deep. Nicole says that her solution is lead-core and small steelhead patterns.

"Woolly Worms, Fall Favorites, Silver Hiltons and other steelhead flies are fine, but use smaller sizes than for steelhead—#8 or even #10. There was a 8 1/2-pound rainbow taken out of Lake Alpine a few years ago and there are still some big fish there."

As with lures, the flies can be trolled with lead-core at various depths until the angler finds where the trout are holding.

For More Information:

Nicole and Peter Cooper, Creekside Sports, 484 E. Highway 4, Murphys, CA 95247, (209) 728-2166. • Maria Tallant, Ebbetts Pass Trading Post, Arnold Plaza, 925 Highway 4, Arnold, CA, (209) 795-1686. • Tom Schachten, Glory Hole Sports, 2892 Highway 49, Angels Camp, CA 95222, (209) 736-4333.

The North Fork of the Stanislaus River downstream from Sourgrass Crossing can be reached with a 10-minute walk from the road and always produces rainbows. Bill Sunderland

Chapter Thirteen

CARSON RIVER

The East Fork of the Carson River tumbles down the eastern slope of the Sierra Nevada, paralleling Highways 4 and 89 for more than six miles and offering numerous opportunities for roadside anglers. At Hangman's Bridge, just before Markleeville, it turns away from the road and becomes a wild trout area.

Along Highway 89 it is mostly park and fish, with bait and lure anglers regularly catching their limit of stocked rainbows. On weekends and holidays particularly, such easy access leads to crowding.

However, an aggressive wader can find bigger fish where the canyon narrows and the road climbs above the river.

The wild trout section of the river that stretches more than 10 miles from Hangman's Bridge near Markleeville to the Nevada border is a different matter. Fishing is restricted to barbless lures and flies with a two-fish, 15-inch minimum limit. There is no easy access—walking or floating the river is the only way to fish it.

When this section of the East Carson was designated a wild trout stream in 1986, fishing was not that good. But it has now come into its own and excellent fishing is available for anglers willing to work their way from the bridge downstream.

There is no other way to do it since no roads go to the Carson until it leaves California. It's rugged country, but the river is large enough so that bankside walking is not all that difficult and a day-long expedition can cover several miles of water. Not many anglers take the trouble, but this stretch of water is steadily improving. The athletic angler can check in Markleeville for current information before deciding if the walk is worth it.

John Sparks, owner of Monty Wolf's Trading Post in Markleeville, describes the fishing as "just miserable" for the first three years after it became a wild trout stream. "The problem," he says, "is that somebody designated it as scenic and wild, meaning you can't stock it."

Bill Sunderland

As a result, he says, it took several years for fish already in that section of the Carson to grow to large size.

Sparks says that Markleeville city fathers hope to get permission to plant some large fish in the wild trout section of the Carson, but that could take several years.

"In the meantime, it has been picking up and I believe that for the first time it is now worth fishing."

Alternatives for anglers wanting to get away from roadside fishing include another stretch of the East Carson which is accessible from Wolf Creek Road. Wolf Creek Road is a clearly marked turnoff to the south from Highway 4 just as the highway and the river join seven miles southwest of Markleeville. For the first mile, the Wolf Creek Road is paved and parallels the river, allowing easy access. For some reason this section of the East Carson is not nearly as heavily fished as the river alongside Highways 4 or 89.

Then Wolf Creek Road climbs and turns to gravel, while the river stays in its canyon. An angler can park and work upstream into the canyon as the road climbs hundreds of feet above it.

Another access to the East Carson is from Wolf Creek Meadows, six miles from the Highway 4 turnoff. As Wolf Creek Road drops into the meadow, a branch to the left leads past some ranch buildings and across the creek to a corral before cutting steeply uphill. A sign says "Dixon Mine, two miles"; in fact the road dead-ends at the Carson River only about a mile away. It's a bumpy, rough mile but can be done without four-wheel drive. The road branches into several fingers just before it reaches the river. All of them end on a bluff a hundred feet above the East Carson.

There are no camping facilities, but there is plenty of level space to camp. Numerous trails lead to the river, so access is no problem.

Just downstream, Wolf Creek enters the Carson. A

number of deep holes make great holding places for bigger trout. It is possible to work downstream all the way to where Wolf Creek Road climbs and leaves the river but it is several miles and a tough hike.

Upstream is just as good for fishing, perhaps even better. The terrain is more difficult and there is more pocket water. The fish throughout this area are wild since it's well away from the stocked sections.

Wolf Creek is stocked in the spring and generally is good fishing, although it can get too low for planting in the late summer and early fall. Instead of turning to the left as Wolf Creek Road enters the meadow, continue straight on and you'll find a campground a mile down the road at the end of the meadow. The creek meanders through the meadow and fishing is fine even though cattle grazing in the meadow have broken down the bank in some places. A better chance for larger trout is to fish upstream from where Wolf Creek enters the meadow.

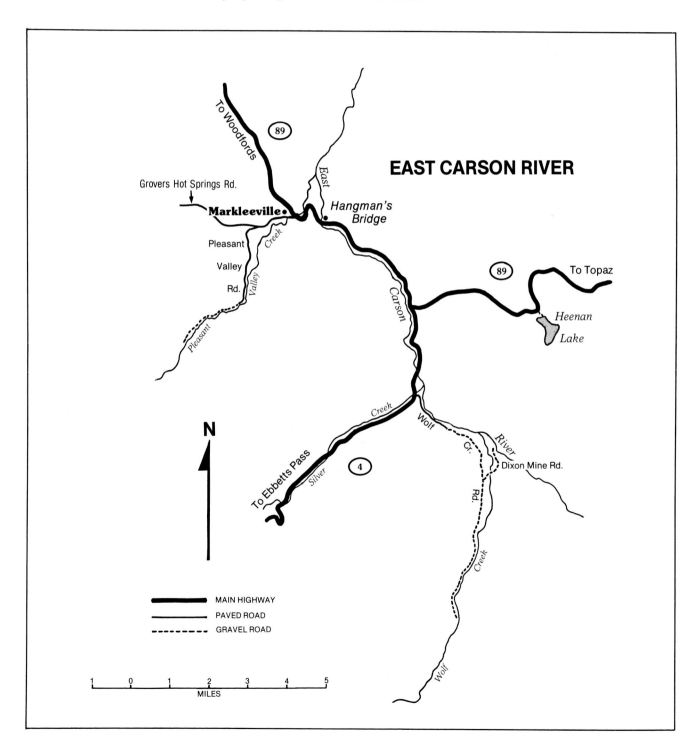

Wolf Creek a half mile above its confluence with the East Carson River near Markleeville can hold some nice trout, but it is difficult fishing in the fall when the water is down. Bill Sunderland

Pleasant Valley

Just three miles from Markleeville is Pleasant Valley, an area reserved for fly fishing. It is a jewel, a pretty, open meadow that allows tangle-free casting for a steady supply of stocked fish along with wily native browns and Lahontan cutthroats. To get there take the road to Grover Hot Springs State Park, which turns north from Highway 89 in the center of Markleeville.

A mile from Markleeville, turn left and follow a road uphill through a housing development and on to the valley. The road is paved through the built-up area, then becomes gravel for the final two miles.

Although current regulations call for fly fishing only with a barbless hook, anglers can keep three fish, with no special size limit. Check the latest DFG sport fishing handbook since there is the possibility that only barbless hooks will be allowed in the future.

Although there are no facilities, there are a number of spots that can be used for camping.

Pleasant Valley offers several types of trout fishing. For the length of the three-mile-long valley, Pleasant Creek snakes back and forth within its deep-cut banks, allowing anglers to fish small riffles, slow-moving runs or a handful of deep pools where dozens of trout are often seen holding in clear water.

Although there are some bankside trees and bushes, for the most part it is open enough to allow casting without worrying about your back cast. It's a great place for the beginning fly fisherman—plenty of fish and wide open spaces.

The road ends less than a half-mile after entering the valley, but the angler who wants to walk upstream can make his or her way through a barbed-wire gate and follow a clearly-marked path. For almost half a mile the path stays within sight of the meandering creek, then cuts through a forested area for another mile and a half, not rejoining the creek until it reaches the far end of the valley. The trail is clear and level, an easy walk.

A favorite way of fishing is to follow the path until it rejoins Pleasant Valley Creek at the head of the valley, then fish back to the parking area. A better part of the day can be spent doing this since for every mile the trail goes the creek doubles the distance as it meanders back and forth.

Another option is to fish the creek upstream from where it rejoins the trail. This leads out of the valley and into a narrow, rugged canyon featuring mostly pocket water. It's excellent fishing but can be tough going.

The third option is to fish Pleasant Valley Creek at the mouth of the valley, where the road from Markleeville enters. As the creek leaves the valley it switches from a meandering spring creek to tumbling rapids and pocket water. Brush closes in and casting becomes much more difficult, but the payoff can be catching brown trout that are half again as big as the stocked rainbows in the meadow section.

John Sparks says that "Pleasant Valley can be the least complicated place to fly fish or it can be the most demanding place because it has every technical aspect you would want. You can go real hard or real easy, and there are a lot of fish there."

On occasion, spawned-out Lahontan cutthroat from Heenan Lake are dumped into Pleasant Valley Creek, and suddenly coming upon a couple of 20-inchers holding at the head of a pool can be disconcerting. Relatively fearless, they often stay in shallow water in plain view until an angler almost steps on them.

The other side of the coin is that there are occasions when it is almost impossible to get them to take any sort of a fly. But it's always exciting to try.

A few native cutthroat also are in the creek, most of them at either end of the valley rather than in the meadow area.

Caddis and mayfly hatches are regular. Royal Wulffs and Humpies in size #12 to #16 are good any time, and Elk Hair Caddis are excellent if there is a hatch. For nymphs, try a #12 Pheasant Tail.

Heenan Lake

Heenan lake is eight miles east of Markleeville on Highway 89 as it leads towards Monitor Pass. The lake, reached by a short, unmarked dirt road that turns south off the highway, is 4.2 miles from the junction of Highways 89 and 4.

Covering 129 surface acres, it sits at 7,200 feet and is surrounded by sagebrush-covered hills still used for summer cattle grazing. Since it was acquired in 1982 by the Wildlife Conservation Board it has been used as the only breeding area in California for Lahontan cutthroat, which are listed as a threatened species.

Heenan Lake was opened to restricted fishing in 1984 to test whether catching and releasing the fish would affect the breeding. Apparently not, it turns out, and so the limited fishing program has continued.

Regulations open the lake only on Friday, Saturday and Sunday from Labor Day through the last Sunday in October. It is barbless hook, no bait, and a strict let-'em-go policy. The entire lake is fenced and a Department of Fish and Game ranger is on hand to collect a $3 entrance fee, which covers the cost of keeping him there during the season.

Prams with electric motors are popular (other motors are not permitted) and can be taken by auto almost to the water down a short access road from the dirt parking lot. But float tubes are the favorite means of fishing the waters, although a number of anglers do well from the bank since the cutthroat tend to hang out in three- to eight-foot water fairly close to shore. The lake itself is not deep, 20 feet at the most.

Heenan Lake is not a garden spot—a couple of portable toilets are the main fixtures. Unless you have a fondness for sagebrush and oak, there's nothing special about the hilly countryside, either. Visitors make the trek for the fishing and nothing else, and the rock-strewn parking lot can get crowded when the bite is on.

And there certainly are fish. An 18-inch cutthroat is normal. It takes a 20-incher for an angler to say with authority that he or she has hooked a fair-sized fish.

The Heenan Lake breeders are a full-bodied fish that are native to the area. According to biologists the strain comes from the pre-historic Lake Lahontan that used to cover a good portion of Nevada, the remnants today of which are Pyramid and Walker lakes. Due to commercial over-fishing late in the last century they died out in Pyramid and became hybridized in most of the remaining areas.

Eggs from the Heenan breeders are distributed to the Hot Creek and Mount Shasta hatcheries. In turn, the grown fish are put into a number of streams and lakes, including Pyramid. Some of the breeding fish also are planted in streams near Heenan, including Pleasant Valley Creek.

There are a lot of Lahontan cutthroat in Heenan and on a good day it is possible to catch and release 10 or more fish, including a number above 20 inches. Fish from 27 to 30 inches aren't unusual. The ranger checks each angler and keeps a log of what was caught, including number and estimated length. A quick look at the log is the best way to determine whether they are biting.

Casting or trolling small flashing lures at a fairly slow speed works best for non-fly fishermen, but flies are the favored means for Heenan.

How many other places can you all but be guaranteed the possibility of catching a trophy-sized trout?

John Sparks of Monty Wolf's Trading Post warns that "some people seem to think that it is a trout pond and you can catch fish with a bare hook. But the fact is you still have to fish the lake."

He adds that "gold colored lures seem to be the best—Kastmasters and Panther Martins—while for flies a black Woolly Bugger is very effective"

Black Woolly Worms sized #8 or #10 take their share of fish, particularly with a red tail to add a spot of color. Smaller nymphs, including the ever-popular Pheasant Tail, also work well. On some days working such a nymph in the surface film very slowly can cause a vicious hit by a big fish. Sparks notes that other effective flies have been grasshoppers and McGintys for dries, along with Montana Stones for wet.

Silver Creek

Silver Creek parallels Highway 4 for almost four miles before it runs into the East Carson. A typical, tumbling Sierra stream, Silver Creek is mostly pocket water and pools. Some of it is easy to get to when the canyon widens, more of it is in a brush-choked gully. Highway 4 crosses the creek several times and John Sparks suggests that one good way to fish it is to work from one bridge up or down stream to the next bridge.

"Personally, it is one of my favorites. I park at the first bridge going towards Ebbetts Pass and fish it up to the next bridge. You can just move from pocket to pocket and fish it all day. It's a very good fly stream, but can be difficult because of the brush and trees.

"It adds to the skill quality of a fisherman."

Silver Creek, Sparks notes, is good until late in the season since unlike many other streams in the area it does not become a thin trickle during August and September.

For More Information:

John Sparks, Monty Wolf's Trading Post, P.O. Box 89, Markleeville, CA 96120, (916) 694-2201.

This is sage brush and juniper country, but the pools of the East Carson are productive. Frank Raymond

Chapter Fourteen

BRIDGEPORT AREA

Want to troll for trophy browns? Cast for rainbows in a fast-moving river? Fly fish in a rippling, crystal-clear creek that holds trout much bigger than have a right to be there? How about hiking? There are plenty of mountain lakes and even one so close that an easy, hour-long walk will put you among four-pound brookies.

Bored with trout? Well, how about casting to grayling. Yup, grayling.

Yeah, but you don't have the money to go to Alaska.

Well, try the Bridgeport area of the eastern Sierra, home of the East and West Walker Rivers, Twin Lakes and myriad other streams. There is so much fishing here, and so many types of fishing, that it is impossible not to find what you like.

Many businesses in Bridgeport live on fishing and the tourism it brings during the summer months. Unlike Mammoth Lakes and the Owens River Valley 35 miles to the south, it does not have a winter ski trade, nor does it lose its best fishing to private ranches that charge for the right to work their streams. It is easily accessible from Southern California by following Highway 395 north, or it can be reached from the Central Valley via Highway 108 through Sonora or Highway 120 through Yosemite Park and over Tioga Pass.

Bridgeport advertises that it has more than 35 lakes and 500 miles of streams within a 15-mile radius of the friendly little town that sits in the middle of a valley devoted mostly to cattle ranching. Many of those lakes and streams are easily accessible by paved road. Campgrounds abound, and family-style amenities are the rule. For anglers who like more privacy, there are a number of areas with fishing and camping that can be reached by gravel or dirt roads.

And, finally, for those willing to shoulder a pack and sleeping bag along with their fishing gear, the selection of high-country streams and lakes is inexhaustible, limited only by stamina and time.

Frank Raymond

Bridgeport Lake and the East Walker River that flows from it are the best-known spots for fishing.

Unfortunately, Bridgeport Lake was all but drained during the 1988-89 drought to provide water to farmers and ranchers in Nevada. Little thought was given to the fish in the East Walker, which were decimated first by the silt flushed into the river as the draw-down neared bottom and then by the lack of water. The 12 miles of the East Walker between the reservoir and the Nevada border are coming back as a trophy trout area, but it may take a few years before fishing reaches its former glory.

In the meantime, the state Department of Fish and Game is considering special restrictions to help in the recovery, so be sure to check before fishing the East Walker since regulations will probably change every year. For some years it has been restricted to barbless flies and lures and a two-trout maximum. Keeper size restrictions are different from the reservoir to the Highway 182 bridge, and from the bridge to the Nevada border. No bait fishing is allowed.

When the season opens in the spring, large streamers, heavy leaders and sinking lines are in order. There are big fish in the East Walker and using fine leaders leaves almost no chance of landing one. So use 1X or even 0X to handle streamers tied on #2 or #4 hooks. Patterns favored locally are black or white Marabou streamers, Woolhead Sculpins, Matukas and just about anything else that imitates minnows.

As summer approaches, switch to large nymphs—Bitch Creek Nymphs are one favorite—that imitate caddis. As the water begins to drop in June and July, the nymph size gets smaller, down to #12s and #14s. Caddis imitations and general patterns such as Zug Bugs are recommended. Hopper patterns fished on top also are effective, particularly in the late summer and fall when weeds sometimes make nymphing difficult.

In October, browns move up to the dam to spawn and at times it seems that every angler in California is there.

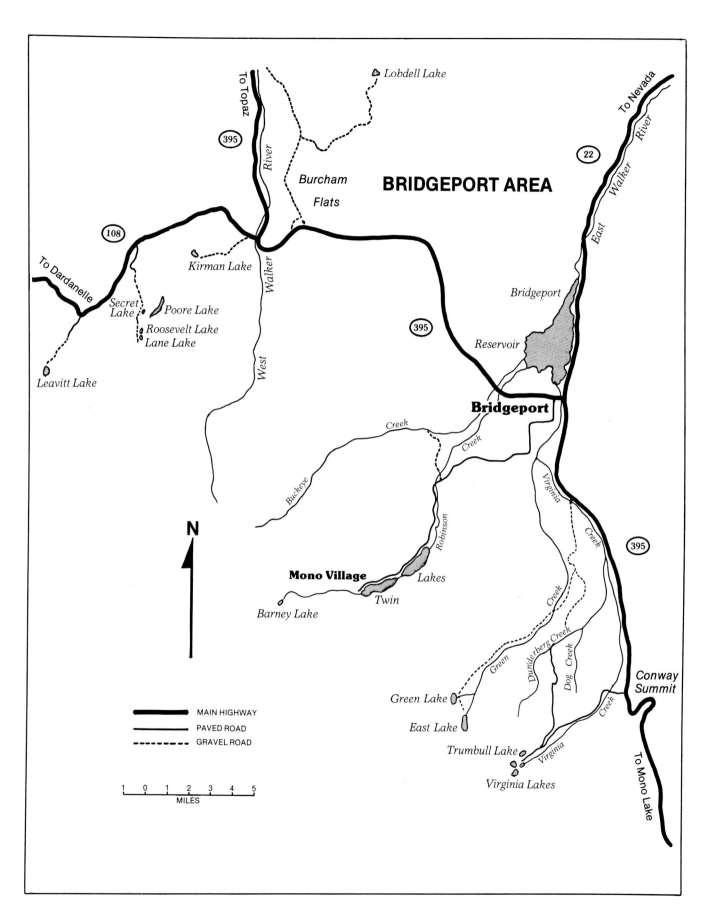

To Topaz

Lobdell Lake

395

22

To Nevada

River

Burcham
Flats

BRIDGEPORT AREA

East Walker River

108

Kirman Lake

Walker

Bridgeport

To Dardanelle

Secret
Lake

Poore Lake

Roosevelt Lake
Lane Lake

West

395

Reservoir

Bridgeport

Leavitt Lake

Creek

Creek

Creek

Buckeye

Virginia

Creek

395

N

Robinson

Mono Village

Lakes

Green

Creek

Dunderberg Creek

Dog Creek

Barney Lake

Twin

Conway
Summit

Green

Green Lake

East Lake

Virginia

To Mono Lake

MAIN HIGHWAY

PAVED ROAD

GRAVEL ROAD

Trumbull Lake

Virginia Lakes

Creek

1 0 1 2 3 4 5
MILES

The "Big Hole" pool just below the dam is almost always jammed with anglers, and with good reason since many of the biggest fish are there. For the mile and a half downstream to the Highway 182 bridge, fly fishermen wanting to wade often have to wait for enough room to cast without cutting into somebody else's territory.

Even fishing in a crowd can be both a pleasure and productive as long as streamside etiquette is followed. But occasionally, bad manners on the part of some anglers make it easier to pick up and fish someplace else. Just remember, the reason this area is so crowded is because it traditionally has been the spot for the biggest fish.

Spin fishermen using lures tend to do the best in the pool just below the dam, while fly fishermen working near banks and other obstructions are more successful on the rest of the river.

The East Walker flows through private land, but the ranchers allow access despite the heavy number of anglers. This courtesy should be repaid by not leaving litter nor bothering the cattle in the fields.

Bridgeport Lake is a large, teardrop-shaped reservoir that holds the waters of the East Walker and several creeks. It is used to control seasonal flow to downstream ranches and farms.

Conway Ranch on the East Fork Walker River. Brad Jackson

Generally shallow except near the dam at the northern end, it can be waded at the southern tip where the East Walker enters. Trophy brown trout and large rainbows are in the lake.

Rick Rockel, owner and manager of Ken's Sporting Goods on Bridgeport's main street, has lived in the area for 25 years. He notes that the reason for Bridgeport Lake's fast-growing trout is because it is so shallow, allowing a rich food source for the fish.

"All the waters that feed into it come down off the drainage from the Sierra, and that water has a chance to warm up," he says. "Bridgeport Lake is full of all sorts of aquatic foods; it has a tremendous minnow population, it has fresh-water snails, fresh-water clams and tremendous insect activity, particularly at the southern (Bridgeport) end of the lake."

Since the lake water is generally murky, fishing with bait or lures rather than flies is more productive. However, Rockel says that there is "the opportunity to catch some big fish float tubing in the dam area in the spring and the fall, using big sculpin patterns or big leach patterns."

Otherwise, he suggests lure fishermen use Rapalas cast off the face of the dam, especially at dusk, in the spring and fall. In the early part of the season, trolling also is excellent, although by mid-July the algae bloom prevents effective trolling. Anglers then switch to bait at the southern end of the lake where the East Walker and the three creeks that feed it come in and cut a path through the weed growth. Trolling resumes late in the season when the algae bloom is over.

Anybody fishing the Bridgeport area for the first time would be well advised to make a stop at Ken's Sporting Goods and talk with Rockel. The well-stocked store opens early and closes late during the fishing season, and the constant flow of anglers in and out brings the latest information on where fishing is best and what they are biting on. Rockel is exact in his directions of how to get to specific fishing areas and what flies, lures or bait to use.

And to whet your appetite, take a peek into the store freezers, which are bound to contain some lunkers that are being kept frozen until they can be taken home by the visiting anglers who caught them.

To describe all of the fishing areas near Bridgeport would be a book in itself, but following are some of the best-known, along with a few that aren't so heavily fished. We will touch on only a few of the many alpine lakes that can be reached by hiking, sticking mostly to the easy-access areas that can be reached by auto or with a short walk. As usual in California, what the angler makes of the fishing depends on the fisherman himself. In many places there are plenty of stocked rainbows a few steps from the car, while a half-mile walk can provide a piece of the stream without company and the thrill of wild trout.

Twin Lakes

Both Upper and Lower Twin Lakes are favorite family fishing areas, boasting a half-dozen well-kept Forest Service campgrounds. There also are stores, rental boats and other facilities both along the lakes and at the privately-owned

The West Walker River high in the Sierra Nevada offers numerous brookies, but only a few are bigger than 8 inches. Ken Hanley crouches as he casts to spooky fish in clear water. Bill Sunderland

Mono Village, located at the end of the 15-mile paved road from Bridgeport that leads to the lakes and then parallels their northern shore. A secondary road circles Lower Twin.

These lakes are much clearer and deeper than Bridgeport Lake—Lower Twin goes to 160 feet and Upper Twin to 120 feet. But the clarity of the water also means that these lakes do not contain the rich nutrients that provide for the fast growth of the Bridgeport trout. That doesn't mean there aren't big trout in Twin Lakes, just not as many. In fact, the state record for a brown—26 pounds, eight ounces, caught in 1987 —was from Upper Twin.

Apart from the browns, there is a regularly-planted population of rainbow trout, along with numerous kokanee. The kokanee are small, six to 11 inches, because the plankton they normally feed on are not present in Twin Lakes. They are easy to catch, particularly in the evening when they come near the surface. Rockel says the most popular and effective lure for kokanee is the Red Magic, although a Dave Davis with a worm also works well.

Both bait and lures cast from the bank will catch rainbows, as will flies during the early mornings and late evenings. Rockel suggests using "the standard double hook, lake rig with Power Bait, Zeke's Floating Bait or Velveeta cheese fished in combination with eggs.

"Throwing lures off the bank also can be very effective. Use wobbling spoons with fluorescent colors, or bubble and fly

fish during the evenings. Typical patterns are Black Gnats and attractors like Royal Wulffs. We also use #8 and #10 Olive Matukas or #8 and #10 Hornberg Specials."

Rockel says that for trolling, which is one of the most popular ways to fish for rainbows, "My favorite is a gold-flecked, light Super Duper or a Jake's Spinner in gold with red dots on it. Other lures also work well, including Mepps, Blue Fox and small Rooster Tails spinners either fished by themselves or with attractor blades." He urges trollers to fish in the early morning or late evening since "that's when you get the least amount of light penetration and the fish are able to come to the surface to feed."

Catching trophy browns in either of the Twin Lakes is tougher and there is little chance of hooking one except by trolling.

"The best time to fish for trophy trout is May and October," Rockel says. "The most popular proven technique for trolling in Twin Lakes is called striker action trolling. We troll at approximately six to eight miles an hour, concentrating on shoreline areas, and we use floating imitation minnow lures such as Rebels or Rapalas.

"In addition to trolling at a high rate of speed, we jig the lure, which imparts a darting action. The theory is that you only want the fish to see the lure momentarily. You want his senses to be awakened, his predatory instincts to take over so he will attack the lure."

Inviting areas such as this are found on many of the small streams in the Bridgeport area. Bill Sunderland

Robinson Creek/Buckeye Creek

Robinson Creek is the outlet for Twin Lakes. It closely follows the road north to Bridgeport for nearly two miles, then meanders off across the valley to end up as a feeder stream for Bridgeport Lake. It is perhaps the most popular of the family fishing areas, with five Forest Service campgrounds, including the big Robinson Creek Campground just a mile from Lower Twin Lake. There is a steady supply of stocked rainbows.

Brown trout also are in Robinson Creek, but catching them is more difficult than picking up hatchery-raised rainbows. The browns are wild and have survived in heavily-fished areas only because they do not readily take the bait or lures to which the planted rainbows fall prey. When they are caught it usually is by a fly fisherman or an angler using a floating Rapala, Rick Rockel says.

For fly fishermen, Rockel says the usual fare on Robinson Creek—and, in fact, on most of the other Bridgeport-area streams—is the Royal Wulff, various caddis patterns, Yellow Humpies, and small Hornberg Specials.

Robinson Creek also is a feeder stream for Upper Twin Lake. An angler can follow a well-marked Forest Service trail from Mono Village at the end of Upper Twin and hike to Barney Lake, about an hour and 15 minute walk upstream. Ideal for a day hike, it contains brook trout in the 8- to 12-inch range that are unsophisticated and easy to catch. Rockel suggests using worms, Power Bait, fly and bubble combinations and small, wobbling spoons and spinners on Barney Lake.

Buckeye Creek is in a drainage to the north of lower Robinson Creek after it exits Lower Twin Lake. It can be reached either by a dirt road that cuts north at Bogards Camp about 2.5 miles north of Twin Lakes on the road to Bridgeport, or on an unimproved dirt road that heads south from the Bridgeport Ranger Station on Highway 395 west of Bridgeport. Several campgrounds on Buckeye Creek offer easy access to fishing.

The lower stretches of Buckeye are planted during the summer, but by working upstream and away from the road an angler can find wild brook trout. There also are some brookies and browns in the lower stretches, along with the planted rainbows.

West Walker River

For fishing purposes the West Walker and East Walker have no relationship. The West Walker tumbles out of the Sierra alongside Highway 108 as it approaches Highway 395. It then parallels 395 north, offering easy-access fishing for a dozen miles before it spills into Antelope Valley and works its way through private land to Topaz Lake on the California-Nevada border.

As a result, most of the fishing is for planted rainbows and a few wild browns. There are several campgrounds on Highway 395 and almost the entire river is fished—and stocked—heavily. One way to avoid the crowds for a morning or afternoon of fishing is to follow the West Walker downstream from the campground-picnic area on Highway 108 about two miles from the junction with 395.

At that point, the West Walker moves away from the highway and cuts northeast through a canyon to intersect with Highway 395 some two miles away. It takes several hours to fish this section of the river and it is a good way to spend a morning or afternoon. Chances of picking up wild trout, including larger browns, are much better since it is not fished nearly as heavily as the other sections of West Walker.

Rick Rockel notes that the West Walker is high in the spring due to snow melt and during a normal year good fishing does not start until mid-June, then lasts through the summer until the season ends.

"The West Walker is easy to fish making it great for kids," Rockel notes. "Typical baits are cheese, worms and salmon eggs. Typical lure patterns there are smaller spinners, particularly spinners with silver blades."

For fly anglers, he suggests the same attractor patterns used on the other eastern Sierra streams, including Yellow Humpies, Royal Wulffs and Hornberg Specials.

After the West Walker enters Antelope Valley, where the towns of Walker and Coleville are located, its character changes to fit the meadowlands through which it flows. And since this meadowland is owned by ranchers and farmers, access is more difficult. Once on the river, anglers can work their way up or down stream but must stay within the high water mark and not step onto private property.

Wading without leaving the water can be worth the trouble since the Antelope Valley portion of the West Walker is home to large brown trout. Rockel points out, however, that "it is susceptible to wild fluctuations of water level due to irrigation practices. Fishing in this area is recommended primarily for experienced fishermen, using large, minnow-type lures such as Rapalas or, late in the season, hopper patterns up on top."

The West Walker feeds into Topaz Lake, which is split by the boundary between California and Nevada. Because of this, like Lake Tahoe, it can be fished with either a California or Nevada fishing license.

There are plenty of rainbows in the 12- to 18-inch range in Topaz and fishing is permitted for most of the year, from Jan. 1 to Sept. 30. Both trolling and still fishing are effective in Topaz.

Rockel says "my favorite lure is the small, floating Rainbow Trout Rapala in a size seven or nine. We also use a lot of Needle Fish in Topaz, trolling them with attractor blades with nightcrawlers behind them.

"Topaz is a great spring and winter fishery for the angler who wants to get out there before the other waters in the eastern Sierra are open," he says.

Kirman Lake

Although locals have known about Kirman Lake (also called Carmen Lake) for years, only recently has it become a favorite spot for visiting anglers. It is the home of brook trout in the four- to six-pound range, along with trophy-sized Lahontan cutthroats, and is ideal for float tubing. Its growing popularity led to a change in restrictions beginning with the 1990 season—no more bait fishing allowed.

The trail to Kirman, actually a dirt road, is off Highway 108 a half-mile from where it intersects Highway 395. Just across a cattle guard there is parking on both sides of the road, and the trail/road can be reached by climbing over a fence on the southern side. The dirt road is on private ranchland and is about a three-mile walk to the lake. A mountain bike will cut the time in half and make it easier to haul along a float tube and other gear.

The best shoreline fishing is in the early and late season —May and October—when the fish are cruising the shoreline or spawning. Otherwise, a float tube is about the only way to pick up good-sized trout.

Walker River brown. Brad Jackson

The setting for the headwaters of the West Walker River, more than 8,000 feet high in the Sierra Nevada near Sonora Pass, is beautiful, but the many brookies are small. Bill Sunderland

Rockel says that "one of the things we know about Kirman Lake that is interesting is that the fish only live to be four years old. They have a tremendous fat buildup on their body which literally gives them heart attacks, just like humans, caused by cholesterol."

The best flies for Kirman, Rockel says, are small Olive Matukas, Spruce Matukas, small leech patterns, Zug Bugs and occasionally freshwater shrimp patterns. The basic food in the lake is shrimp, "but by fishing shrimp patterns you are competing with millions of naturals. As a result, we found that other patterns work best."

For lure fishermen, he recommends fluorescent silver spoons, including Panther Martins and Rooster Tails.

Highway 108

A few miles west on Highway 108 from the Kirman Lake trail is Leavitt Meadow, a jumping-off point for easy hikes to a series of lakes that offer fine trout fishing. Just south of Leavitt Meadow Lodge is a campground with convenient roadside parking for anglers who want to walk in to Poore Lake, Lane Lake, Roosevelt Lake and Secret Lake.

All four lakes are within an hour and a half walk, even less if you use a mountain bike. Poore Lake is the largest, but all offer a variety of trout.

Poore lake, like Kirman, has trophy brook trout in the four- to five-pound range and Kamloops strain rainbows that run nearly as big. The three smaller lakes have brook and Lahontan cutthroat trout that run up to a couple of pounds in size.

Rockel suggests Power Bait, cheese baits, nightcrawlers, worms and salmon eggs for these lakes, while the best lure patterns are "yellow bodied spinners, particularly with silver blades, and wobbling spoons with fluorescent stripes." He suggests nymphs such as Zug Bugs or Gold Ribbed Hare's Ears for flies, along with leech patterns, which seem to work even in areas where there are no leeches.

A main food for the big brookies in Poore Lake are Lahontan redside suckers.

"To imitate them," Rockel says, "we use gold spoons with fluorescent stripes and/or streamer patterns such as a multi- colored Marabou Muddler that contains some red and some gold. The big brook trout feed on these suckers early in the morning and late in the evening when they corral them on the shallow shelves that surround the lake." He notes that the other lakes are deeper, pot-hole type lakes so those patterns are not as effective on them.

Some 10 miles up Highway 108, nearly to the Sierra crest, a four-wheel drive road strictly for high-centered vehicles leads to Leavitt Lake. The lake has great brook trout and kamloops fishing, but at 9,500 feet it is cold and generally iced over until late June or early July. Because it is deep, bait fishing is the best bet for anglers, although occasionally flies can be effective in the early morning or late evening.

Highway 395 South

There also are a number of fishing areas on or near Highway 395 south of Bridgeport. The farthest south is a group of lakes—Little Virginia, Big Virginia and Trumbull—easily accessed by way of an eight-mile-long dirt road that turns southwest off the highway at Conway Summit.

The lakes are heavily stocked with both rainbow and brook trout and there are some wild browns. There are campgrounds both on the lakes and on Virginia Creek, which follows the road to Highway 395. Easy access means the entire area is heavily fished.

The lakes are at about 9,500 feet and normally inaccessible until early or mid-June. Some locals go up earlier when the road has been plowed and use them for ice fishing.

Bait is the most effective way to fish the lakes, although bubble and fly combinations or wobbling spoons also work.

Several other lakes are only a 15-minute hike away, but they are not stocked and the trout generally are stunted due to lack of food.

Virginia Creek drops into a gorge as it parallels Highway 395 towards Bridgeport, but it still is accessible and can be good fishing for anybody willing to do a little hiking. The same holds true eight miles south of Bridgeport, where Dog Creek and Dunderberg Creek flow into Virginia Creek.

The down timber and beaver ponds can make it tough going in spots, but the reward is larger browns, along with big rainbows and brookies.

Closer to Bridgeport, after Green Creek has joined the flow, the stream becomes more accessible and is stocked. However, for some reason anglers tend to pass it by, so despite the easy access it can be a productive place to fish.

Green Creek itself is accessible by a dirt road and offers some three miles of roadside fishing. It is excellent for fly anglers and is one of Rick Rockel's favorite spots. But he warns that the clear water and educated fish can make it tough.

"Success is limited to angling skill. I recommend that high skill level fishermen concentrate on Green Creek," he says. "It is not a good place for the average family to fish because of the clarity of the water and the spookiness of the fish."

The turnoff to Green Creek is an unmarked dirt road West off Highway 395 just as it begins to drop into the Bridgeport valley. The road forks after a mile, with a sign showing Green Creek to the left. After another mile and a half, the road forks again with a hard, uphill turn to the right leading to Green Creek. A few hundred yards further along is a pond.

From there upstream the road parallels the creek, which is shaded by aspen and other trees and brush. There also is a meadow where the creek has been slowed by beaver ponds.

Rockel says that "patterns I like to fish on Green Creek are small, black flying ants in size #16, attractor patterns like a Royal Wulff or Yellow Humpy, size #16, or caddis or mayfly patterns in size #14 and #16. Typically, the caddis patterns have an olive thorax and the mayflies are cream-colored, such as the Light Cahill or Pale Morning Dun."

At the end of the road is a campground, which also is the trailhead for three popular lakes—Green Lake, East Lake and West Lake. They all contain rainbows, browns and brookies, some of them quite large. East Lake and Green Lake are the most popular, with good bait fishing or lure fishing throughout the summer.

In October, West Lake is noted for 16- to 20-inch brown trout, usually taken on large, gold wobbling spoons. Smaller fish are available in all three lakes throughout the season and Rockel says they'll bite "on any technique you like."

Lobdell Lake

Fourteen miles north of Bridgeport on Highway 395 is a turnoff to the east marked "Burcham Flats/Lobdell Lake." About four miles along the road a branch to the right eventually leads to Lobdell Lake, a man-made reservoir with a thriving population of Montana grayling.

As the summer wears on the lake becomes little more than an oversized mud puddle and the hungry grayling are enthusiastic about taking whatever you want to toss at them.

Rockel says that "this lake is a great confidence booster for the novice fly fisherman or somebody who wants to fish with a fly and a bubble. We typically use size #16 and #18 AP Black Nymphs, or any small black dry or wet fly.

"I've been up there in the fall and you can literally catch a fish on every cast."

For More Infromation:

Rick Rockel, Ken's Sporting Goods, Main Street, Bridgeport, CA 93517, (619) 932-7707.

Road to Lobdell Lake. Bill Sunderland

Chapter Fifteen

OWENS RIVER

I've been told for years, "The eastern slope of the Sierra, has more and bigger trout than any place else in California."

There's an easy way to prove it—fish the Owens River Valley area near Mammoth Lakes. Both the Owens River and Hot Creek are nutrient-rich spring creeks that hold an amazing number of big fish. And they empty into Crowley Lake, which is noted for its trophy trout.

In 1985, The California Department of Fish and Game conducted an electroshock survey of both streams and found more than 11,000 fish per mile in each of

Brad Jackson

them. For the record, biologists don't pump electricity through a whole mile of a stream or river, they do it in a measured area they consider representative water and then work out how many fish that would be for a mile.

At Hot Creek, they turned up 10,018 browns and 1,396 rainbows per mile, for a total of 11,414 fish. For the Owens River, it was 2,262 browns and 8,785 rainbows for a total of 11,047. The fish came in all sizes, but with plenty of big ones.

That's the good news. The bad news is that there isn't much of either stream open to public access. What is open is limited to barbless fly or lure fishing with size and limit restrictions during the time of the year when the big trout are there.

Much of both streams is in private hands—two fishing ranches and a private club on the Owens and one fishing ranch on Hot Creek. The ranches allow only paying guests to fish their section of the water.

On the Owens above Crowley Lake are Alper's Owens River Ranch and Arcularius Ranch, both with cabins available at reasonable prices. Hot Creek Ranch, on Hot Creek, is a bit more expensive but offers somewhat better accommodations. All three are heavily booked in advance and all three have restrictions on their fishing.

Owens River Ranch and Arcularius Ranch allow fly

fishing only, and it is all barbless hook, catch and release. Hot Creek Ranch is the same with an added caveat, dry flies only. When the ranch was sold years back it was with a clause that only dry fly fishing would be allowed on its waters.

That can be frustrating when guests can see 20-inch browns nymphing on the bottom and can't move them up top to take dries. But nobody ever said fly fishing was supposed to be easy.

Trout in both the Owens and Hot Creek are mostly wild. Stocking occurs in public areas only in mid-summer when the big trout from Lake Crowley are not in the streams to spawn. During that period the regulations change and fishing becomes mostly a put-and-take situation.

Hot Creek runs into the Owens River, which in turn feeds Crowley Lake, a large reservoir that sends its water downstream to Los Angeles. There also is good fishing and much easier public access on the Owens below Crowley and it doesn't carry the restrictions that exist above the reservoir. On the other hand, it doesn't have so many trophy fish, either.

The Mammoth Lakes area, part of the Inyo National Forest, is a rich fishery with numerous lakes and streams. Many of them are stocked and anglers who prefer to use bait or like to eat their catch can fish just about any type of water they want. There's a good variety of camping and hiking, too, along with spectacular scenery.

The Owens River Valley, which runs through the middle of the national forest, is 7,000 feet high and is roughly the same distance from Los Angeles as it is from San Francisco.

Owens River

The headwaters of the Owens are at Big Springs, just two miles off Highway 395 along Owens River Road. Owens River Road is a clearly marked turnoff to the east seven miles north of Mammoth Lakes. Big Springs is a public campsite and fishing is open to the public for about a mile downstream, until it hits Alper's Owens River Ranch. Regulations are two fish, 18 inches or larger, barbless lures or flies, from opening day through June 30, and then through the month of October until closing. In between, the limit is the same as the general state regulations and the DFG does stock the river.

(NOTE: Always check regulations since they can change year by year. Where special regulations exist at the time of writing they are mentioned so anglers not interested in that type of fishing won't be surprised to find such restrictions when they get there.)

It is only about a dozen air miles from Big Springs to Crowley, but the Owens is a meandering meadow stream that with all its loops and twists covers close to 30 miles. Throughout the fishing season it is clear and clean, even though there is some snow melt in the spring. Its water level varies little and the smorgasbord of caddis, stoneflies, mayflies and midges allow trout to grow quickly to trophy size.

It's a typical example of an excellent spring creek and the same abundance of food and clear water that allow trout growth also make it demanding fishing. Owens River trout see plenty of artificials and have the time to inspect an angler's offerings before taking them. As a result, long

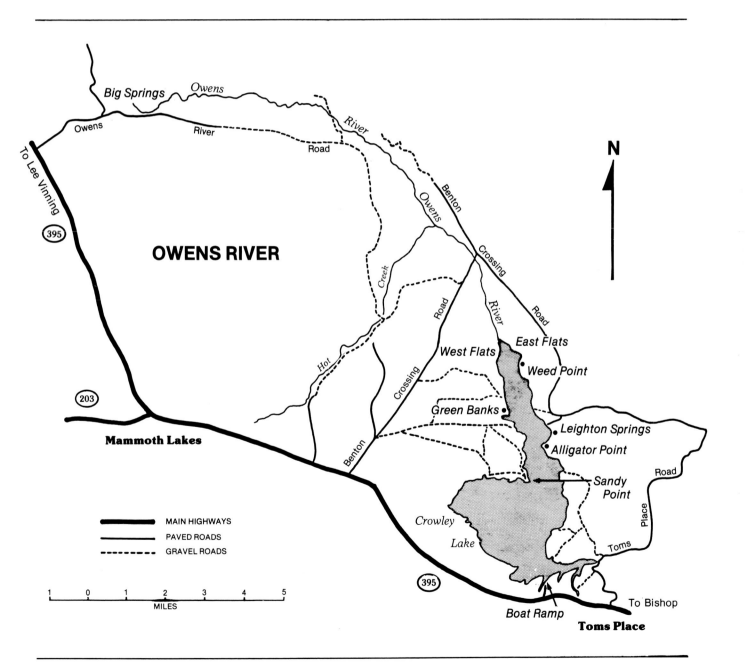

The Owens River, shown here on the privately-owned Arcularius Ranch, is one of the few spring creeks in California. Bill Sunderland

leaders, pinpoint casts with drag-free drifts and match-the-hatch flies are a must.

Another difficulty is the wind. Although it tends to drop in late afternoon and evening, there are days when there is almost no letup and tangled leaders and wind knots are the norm for everybody but the expert.

Finally, most of the surrounding countryside is meadow, so creeping on hands and knees to get into position to cast to a spooky rainbow can pay off. Remember, if you can see them then they can see you, so the less of yourself that shows above the bank, the better chance you have of catching a lunker rather than simply saying good-bye as it torpedoes downstream.

There's less than a mile of public access from Big Springs to the Alper's Owens River Ranch. The ranch has about a mile and a half of stream and borders on the Arcularius Ranch, which owns almost five miles of Owens River bankside. It was on Arcularius Ranch where the DFG shocked the stream to measure the trout population in 1985.

The ranch, owned and run by the Arcularius family since it became a fishing ranch in 1919, has fewer than 20 cabins. Most of the cabins are large, with two or three bedrooms, and are fine for a group of anglers. Even at capacity there's enough room on the ranch to comfortably fish a stretch of the stream without feeling crowded. The entire river has easy access, allowing anglers to drive their cars to whatever spot they like.

The ranch continues to run more than 100 head of cattle, including several bulls, and although they feed along the river they have not broken down the banks as has been done to some other creeks where cattle run free. It can be disconcerting to look over your shoulder and see a bull behind you, but it quickly becomes obvious that they are used to seeing people.

"They see so many fishermen that they can probably suggest what type of fly to use," jokes John Arcularius, who now runs the ranch.

Downstream, there is a private fishing club and then the Frank Arcularius ranch, both of which are closed to the public. But below that the Owens River is open to the public (with the same restrictions as at Big Springs) on down to where it feeds into Crowley. It is about five miles as the crow flies but double that walking the stream bank.

There are two ways to get to the Owens. The first is to follow Owens River Road for almost five miles past the Arcularius Ranch. Just past a cattle gate is a dirt road to the left that goes to the river. A second and easier way is via Benton Crossing, a paved road that can be reached from Highway 395. It crosses the Owens about a mile upstream from where it enters Crowley.

The Owens River from Big Springs to Crowley, whether on public or private land, is fished the same way. The stream, the fish and the insects are the same and big trout are everywhere.

Fred Rowe, a guide and instructor in Mammoth Lakes,

has been fishing and guiding in the area since 1981. With a degree in fisheries biology from Humboldt State University, Rowe is more inclined than most fishermen to make a detailed study of the entomology and patterns of the rivers and streams, and his knowledge pays off.

"The first thing on the Owens," he says, "is that you have to look at what kind of fishing it is. It's a migratory fishery—what's happening is that fish come out of Crowley to spawn.

"There are three runs of fish that come into the river: rainbows in the spring, and again in the fall since the Hot Creek Hatchery has developed a fall-spawning rainbow. The browns also spawn in the fall. In between those two times it is basically a rookery type fishery.

"In other words, it's like a steelhead stream—when they are spawning you have real big fish to fish for, but the rest of the time there are only juvenile fish."

Rowe says that in a normal year the big fish spawn in the headwaters of the Owens near Big Springs when the season opens in late April. During a heavy-weather year they might run a week or so late.

He recommends fishing nymphs along the entire public area from Big Springs to Alper's Ranch, with Gold Ribbed Hare's Ears size #12 or #14 his favorite, along with Pheasant Tails or various types of caddis imitations.

"We also fish a Peacock Woolly Bugger, which is a Black Woolly Bugger with a peacock herl body, in about a size #10 or #12, like a nymph or a streamer," Rowe adds.

Within weeks, anglers can switch to dries and score on the big fish by using the classic Fall River drift technique, with long leaders and absolutely no drag.

After spawning, along about the middle or the end of May, the big fish start moving downstream again to return to Crowley. It's then that the fishing picks up on the private ranches, or in the public stretch that empties into the lake.

At that point, Rowe says, "Use sinking lines, fishing big streamers or nymphs up underneath the cut banks. Olive Matukas or Woolly Buggers in olive or black, size #4 to #8, are what I use the most.

"There are two ways to fish during this period—you either have to get flies down deep and into the holes, or you can strip them in and out of the cut banks and get the fish to come out and take them. The problem with fishing this section of the river is that it is real hit and miss because you have to find the fish. They are not podded up, so the trick is to cover a lot of territory to find one or two big fish.

"You cast and you cover the water, get the flies down deep. If you don't get anything, keep going. Cast and move, cast and move."

By the Fourth of July most big fish have returned to Crowley and although the action on dries becomes fast and furious on the Owens most of the fish are 10 inches or less. In October, when the browns and rainbows again are spawning, they come out of Crowley and begin to work their way upriver. Rowe says "one of the best ways to fish the Owens is to have somebody drop you off at Benton Crossing and then pick you up at the lake. Walk the whole

Ray Austin fishing the Owens River on the Arcularius Ranch. Bill Sunderland

way down. It's a good day's fishing but it is a hell of a way to cover the river."

As the fish work their way upriver, they move onto the ranches, and if an angler hasn't booked the year before it is tough finding room during this period. They eventually will hit Big Springs once again as the season draws to a close. But remember, it's about 7,000 feet elevation and can get cold, with snow flurries not unheard of.

HOT CREEK

The best way to start fishing Hot Creek is to stop by the Hot Creek Hatchery just off Highway 395 and take a look at the thousands of 20-inch (and larger!) trout in the holding pens. That way you won't feel so overwhelmed the first time you spot three or four rainbows that size holding in the creek.

There isn't much of Hot Creek to fish, but what there is can be tremendous. Below the hatchery, a bit more than two miles of the stream belongs to the Hot Creek Ranch, a private ranch that offers dry fly fishing for guests who book its nine cabins. The creek meanders through an open meadow and in the clear water the fish are easy to spot. Catching them is a different matter—long leaders, sneaky tactics and accurate casting are necessary.

Below the ranch .9 of a mile of the stream is open to the public. Then hot water pours into the creek from thermal springs, wiping out the fishing from there until Hot Creek enters the Owens River above Crowley Lake. The hot water keeps the big fish in Hot Creek so they don't migrate to Crowley Lake for part of the season.

The public access section of Hot Creek is one of the most heavily-fished stretches of water in California. It is limited to barbless flies and is strictly catch-and-release. The walk down to the river from two small parking areas on the

Flanked by volcanic cliffs, Hot Creek flows through a lovely canyon that marks the lower third of Hot Creek Ranch as well as the public section of no-kill public water. Brad Jackson

dirt road that parallels Hot Creek is fairly steep, but it is only a hundred yards long. The stream itself maintains the same meadow style as on the ranch upstream.

The public access section does not have the same dry-fly restriction as on the ranch and early in the season nymphs are particularly effective.

Fred Rowe teaches a number of beginning fly fishing classes and delights in taking students to Hot Creek where they can spot monster fish. He says that "in the spring, mayflies and caddis flies make up the bulk of the nymphs. Use Hare's Ear, Pheasant Tail, or the AP series in olive, cream or black. There are even a few patterns developed in the area, such as the Burlap Caddis, which work real well. Another fly is a Chamois Nymph, made of chamois material tied as a caddis imitation.

"As hatches begin, one of the first is the classic baetis mayfly, a blue and olive type. So we use blue duns, parachutes, and then into caddis, both dark and light. We use Elk Hair for light caddis, as well as Kings River Caddis parachutes. For dries, use #16 and smaller, and for nymphs, #12s to #16s."

Rowe says that "another fly we do real well with that most people don't think to use is a #4 Olive Woolly Bugger. This blows a lot of people away, but it has become one of my favorite flies on Hot Creek.

"You cast them as far as you can, then strip them in a way that makes them work the structure, right through the holes in the weed beds. You have to have polarized sun glasses and good eyes because three-quarters of the hits you never even know you have them.

"The fish come in and taste the flies, generally the tail. You have to throw the rod tip down so it drifts into their mouth, and then they smash it. Otherwise they'll just chase it across the river."

Rowe believes that Hot Creek fishes best from the opener to the middle of July. From then on the weeds have built up so much that feeding lanes are reduced to three or four inches, and to fish it with a dry fly the angler needs to be able to handle 20 feet of leader.

CROWLEY LAKE

Fishing Crowley is a must for every California angling enthusiast. Although it is a planted lake, the rate of growth is so fast that seven-inchers dumped in May will be 15 inches in October. And it is so big that many of the trout live for years to become five or more pounds.

Although Crowley boasts mayflies and caddis as part of its food chain, midges and perch minnows play the major role. At certain times of the year, fishing the weed growth along the banks, where big trout are feeding on perch minnows, can be exhilarating. Although best fished from a float tube, anglers also can work from the bank.

Crowley has two distinct seasons—until the end of July, when regulations are open, and from Aug. 1 until Oct. 31, which is the trophy season and regulations limit anglers to barbless lures and flies, with a two-trout limit of 18 inches or bigger.

Although many anglers don't fish Crowley until the trophy season, Fred Rowe of Sierra Bright Dot says he finds it worthwhile from opening day on. He notes, however, that there are a number of boaters on the lake, so float tube fishermen need to be careful. One way he suggests is to fish near the mouth of the Owens River, which enters Crowley at its northern end. Fishing there is excellent and it is shallow enough so that most boaters stay away.

"Early in the year it is mostly blind fishing or trolling," Rowe says. "Sometimes you can see pods of fish working and get to them. The areas around Alligator Point and Leighton Springs are hot spots, and Sandy Point is usually real good. Green Banks also can be good."

If you want a break from trout fishing, Rowe says that in May and June the Sacramento perch come into the shallows to spawn. Fishing for them can be fun, not to mention the opportunity to catch a fine-eating fish.

"They reproduce in such a way so that you can't really over-fish them. It's nothing to have 50 to 100 fish days. Off of Green Banks you can get perch two or three pounds," he says.

By August, the perch fry are big enough to imitate with lures and that's when fishing for the big trout that chase them into the bankside weed beds becomes exciting. But since they are in shallow water they are spooky, so long, accurate casts are necessary to avoid putting them down.

"Using a float tube, work around the weed beds. Once you find the fish, stay on them. We check areas we know are hot spots and we troll around until we see working fish, and then we start after them," Rowe says.

He also notes that as the minnows become bigger, the big fish take them harder and harder. "We used to fish 4X leader, but 70 percent of the fish go right through them. I finally settled on 1X or 2X since the fish aren't really leader shy. You don't need the heavy leaders to land the fish but to sustain the weight of the original hit. Even so, I still get fish that break the leader like it wasn't there."

Crowley also has caddis and midge hatches in the fall. Although working caddis imitators near the Owens can be productive, the midge hatch is so prolific that Rowe says it isn't much use trying to use an artificial to compete with the millions of naturals.

ACCESS

The best road to both the western and eastern banks of Crowley is Benton Crossing Road, which turns east off Highway 395 just south of the Mammoth/June Lake Airport. Both the second and third roads turning off to the right lead to the lake. (The first turnoff at the Green Church does not go to Crowley). The second turnoff, at Whitmore Hot Springs, forks after a little more than half a mile. If you stay left from there on you'll end up at the Green Banks section of Crowley Lake, which is good fishing all year around.

Other turnoffs along that road all lead to the lake, but if you keep to the right forks you'll find yourself at Sandy Point.

The third turnoff is just beyond a cattle guard a bit over three miles from Highway 395. It turns into a honeycomb of roads as it approaches Crowley, with the southernmost ending at Green Banks and the northernmost at the West Flats.

To reach the eastern side of the lake, continue along Benton Crossing Road until it crosses the Owens River then turn right .7 of a mile from the bridge. This dirt road goes to the Owens and then splits. Right leads to the upper Owens, left follows the lake shore to East Flats, Weed Point and Leighton Springs. Alligator Point, one of the best fishing areas on Crowley, is about a mile south of where the road ends.

The western side of the southern end of Crowley can be reached by following Highway 395 south until a clearly-marked turnoff leads to several bays. This is a boat-launch area and has camping facilities.

To get to the eastern side of southern Crowley, continue a bit further south on Highway 395 and then take the road to Toms Place, which crosses Crowley at the dam. A dirt road where 4-wheel drive is advisable turns off to the left and offers a number of access points. The Toms Place road also allows access to the Owens River gorge below the dam.

For More Information:
Fred Rowe, Sierra Bright Dot, P.O. Box 9013, Mammoth Lakes, CA 93546, (619) 934-5514.

Arid, high-desert sage slopes contrast with the lush green riparian zone along the spring-fed Owens River. Trout number over 11,000 per mile in the fertile water upstream from Lake Crowley. Brad Jackson

Chapter Sixteen _____

KINGS RIVER

I n March or early April, when spring has warmed the air and it's time to get back to the mountains, it would be great to toss a line into a rushing stream and pull out a few trout. But the general season is closed until late April and fishing lakes and reservoirs just isn't the same thing.

However, there IS salvation! It comes in the form of an excellent trout stream that is open to fishing all year around—the Kings River, tucked into the western slope of the Sierra Nevada in Central California southeast of Fresno.

Fishing pressure on this river is never heavy. Southern Californians tend to go to the eastern slope of the Sierra, while Northern Californians trek to the many fishing areas around Tahoe, or head for the Upper Sacramento, McCloud River or Hat Creek. And the Central Valley folks who do fish the Kings are smart enough not to tell the rest of California how good it is and thereby bring in the crowds.

This lack of pressure is the reason the Department of Fish and Game allows trout fishing all year. It also is the reason they don't stock the river, so fishing is for wild trout. While the fish generally don't match the size of those that populate many of the Sierra eastern slope waterways, there still are a lot of browns and rainbows in the 20-inch range.

During summer the weather can be hot enough to be miserable. Fall probably offers the best and most comfortable fishing, but early spring, before the snow melt turns the river into a torrent, can be productive.

While fishing some parts of the Kings is possible all winter, snow precludes fishing other sections. In the areas that are accessible, the water gets cold enough that trout become lethargic and hard to catch.

The result is sort of a good news/bad news situation—the river is there, it is open all year, it has fish in it and there is little pressure. But fishing it during most of the period when no other streams are open generally isn't the best time

Frank Raymond

for catching trout.

The Kings River, for fishing purposes, can be broken into three sections—below Pine Flat Reservoir, directly above Pine Flat Reservoir and near Cedar Grove in the Kings Canyon National Park. Each section has different characteristics, but the sections just above and below Pine Flat Reservoir are the only areas that can be reached in winter since they are well below the snow level.

The Cedar Grove area is at a much higher elevation and the road is not kept open when snow begins to fall.

Below Pine Flat Reservoir

The eight-mile stretch of the Kings River from Piedra downstream to Minkler used to be a fantastic fishery for 14-to 20-inch rainbows, but it has yet to recover from a fish kill several years ago. There still are big, eager fish lurking in the riffles and deep pools—just not as many of them.

Except for the area bordered by orange groves and farms, it is easy to access, with two public parks on the river. There are roads on both sides of the Kings, Trimmer Springs Road on the north and Piedra Road on the south. They both lead to Piedra, where a bridge crosses the Kings and where public fishing ends since the river then moves onto private property.

The easy access also means this is where fishing pressure is the heaviest, particularly on weekends. Most of the pressure, however, is from locals who toss bait into the river and wait for something to happen. Aggressive fly anglers or spin fishermen still can take large trout just about anyplace.

A favorite area, particularly for fly fishermen, is behind Avocado Park, which is on the southern bank a couple of miles downstream from Piedra bridge. One feature of the park is a stocked pond where fishing pressure is heavy. But the Kings flows behind the pond only a hundred feet away and a

92

dirt road leads from either end of the park to the river and the back side of the pond.

At the eastern end of the park, where the dirt road joins the river, is a large slick that during evening hatches can be dimpled with rising trout. Whether it can be waded depends on how high the flow is from Pine Flat Reservoir to feed the needs of farmers and ranchers in the Central Valley.

This holds true for the entire stretch, so check carefully before attempting to wade, particularly as the summer wears on and more water is moving through the river.

Caddis are the main hatch in the area, and Kings River Caddis, particularly the parachute version, is effective in a #12 through #16.

Another popular section is just below Piedra bridge, where the river moves quickly around and over boulders that make great holding areas for big fish.

Above Pine Flat Reservoir

From Piedra bridge, Trimmer Springs Road leaves the river and winds up to and around Pine Flat Reservoir. It is a 25-mile drive around the many arms of the reservoir to reach the Kings River as it enters the lake. One of the arms is Big Creek, which can also be fished upstream from where the road crosses, or downstream when the reservoir is down in low water years.

The best area to fish the Kings is upstream from where Trimmer Road crosses the south fork for the second time—a one-lane bridge. The paved road doubles back, but dirt roads on either side of the river allow easy access both for fishing and camping. The road on the northern side of the Kings, the far side of the bridge coming from Pine Flat Lake, dead-ends after seven miles at Garnet Dike Camp.

This is a favorite putting-in spot for spring and early summer rafters, who in high-water years make this stretch of the river a busy spot during the day and can be disruptive to anglers. However, by late afternoon, when feeding activity generally picks up, the rafters normally are off the river.

The dirt road that follows the southern side of the Kings has several campgrounds within several miles and also offers easy river access until it dead-ends.

The fishing is the same from either side—riffles, holes and long tail-outs. A lot of big fish are in the river here, but they didn't get big by being easy to catch. This is a spot for

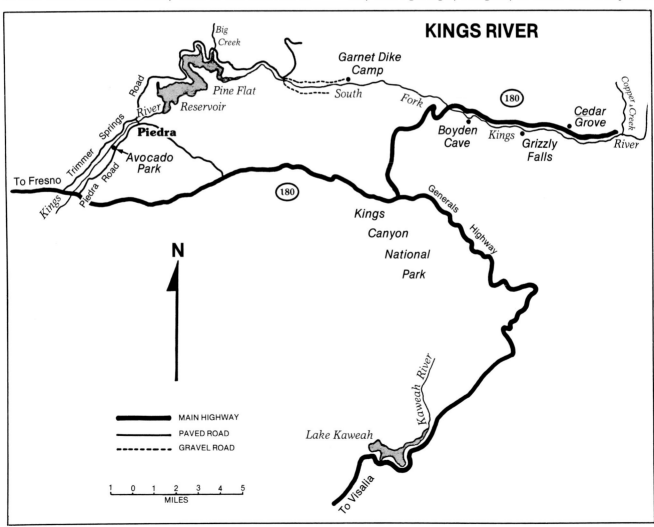

the serious angler, particularly for the fly fisherman who likes to work nymphs or streamers.

This is the area where excellent fishing is available in early spring, before the regular season opens. If the weather is warm enough, this section of the river can provide trout of steelhead size. Although a few campers are around on nice weekends, it is almost deserted on weekdays.

A lot depends on the water temperature—if it is too cold, then raising the big trout from the pools can be tough. This entire area is a wild trout fishery, which is one reason the fish are so big.

About the time the season opens, the snow melt makes the river too high and too cold for good fishing. But fishing picks up again in the summer.

The only drawback during early summer is that this area is close enough to the Central Valley to be hot.

From Garnet Dike Camp, the Kings is not accessible by road until it picks up Highway 180 near Boyden Cave in the Sequoia National Forest nearly 10 miles upstream.

Upper Kings River

Larry Goates, manager of Buz's Fly Shop in Visalia, says that the upper Kings River in Kings Canyon National Park "is the best fishery on the west side of the Sierra." Goates, a native of Visalia who has guided in the area for years, says the river is incredibly prolific. "What the river lacks in sizeable fish it makes up in quantity," he says, adding that "it is hard not to catch fish here."

From where Highway 180 drops into the canyon and picks up the river at Boyden Cave to where it dead-ends at Copper Creek is about 10 miles, with Cedar Grove Village at mid-point. From Boyden Cave to Cedar Grove the river rushes through the canyon, providing only fast-water fishing that makes it tough for fly anglers until late in the summer when the water level drops. However, from Cedar Grove to Copper Creek, the river slows considerably, offering much easier fishing.

Copper Creek is a major trailhead, with long-term parking for hikers headed into the back country. It also is an excellent jumping-off spot for anglers to work upstream to where Bubb's Creek enters the Kings, an easy two-mile hike.

Goates recommends fishing from Cedar Grove upstream early in the summer, as soon as the runoff is low enough to allow. There is no planting on the Kings—it is a wild trout area—which means that bait fishing can be less productive than with planted areas.

A two-trout limit also discourages fishing for many anglers. As a result, even in the area near the Cedar Grove campgrounds, fly anglers can find excellent action early in the summer, particularly with smaller fish.

For the record, like the lower Kings River this section is open to fishing year around, but the road is not kept open in the winter when snowfall begins.

Goates says that from Cedar Grove upstream the river "yields extremely well to the fly, but not to the spin

fisherman. This is one of the worst spin-fishing rivers because it is shallow and wide—the average depth is probably around two or three feet." For bait anglers, he recommends the Grizzly Falls area about three miles downstream from Cedar Grove.

As with many rivers, this section of the Kings offers different fishing possibilities at different times of the year.

After fishing the Cedar Grove to Bubb's Creek area during the early summer, Goates says that "starting in August I start going downstream and fishing along the road. It's rougher down there, not meadowy as it is upstream. But from Grizzly Falls to Boyden Cave the fish get bigger, averaging 10 inches and getting up to 15 or 20 inches. Most of the big fish are browns, but two of the biggest I've seen were rainbows."

Goates says that "hatches on the Kings are not prolific. Caddis hatches are sporadic throughout the year; large salmon flies happen in late May and June. In June there are some larger mayfly species and during that period fishing can be non-stop. I've hooked 30 or 40 fish in two hours during an evening—one every cast."

On Oct. 1 the store at Cedar Grove closes and the visitor level drops drastically. It's then, Goates says, that the area offers the best fishing, even though it is surrounded by campgrounds. It's that area he fishes until snow closes the road.

"I use attractor patterns, with a preference for the Western Coachman. It can be swung wet style and take fish or be greased and fished dry. There are some times of year when you get small, cream mayflies coming off and a Royal Wulff isn't going to catch as many as a #16 Light Cahill. But for the most part throughout the year if you have something like an Elk Hair Caddis or Coachman or Wulff, it's fine."

He recommends #10s through #16s—"I've never needed to use anything smaller than a #16 on this river."

Kaweah River

Another off-season area worth fishing is the Kaweah River above Lake Kaweah, on Highway 198 less than 20 miles southeast of Visalia. In December and January large trout move out of the lake and into the river to spawn. This is a time when locals crowd the area and pressure is heavy but fruitful.

Eggs and Power Bait are effective for bait fishermen, while Woolly Worms or Woolly Buggers are the best for fly anglers. In most cases careful walking of the bank, which can be easily accessed from a number of points, means spotting big fish holding at the heads of riffles. Blind casting doesn't do much good; it's necessary to find a fish and work it carefully.

For More Information:
Larry Goates or Mickey Powell, Buz's Fly Shop, 219 N. Encina, Visalia, CA 93291, (209) 734-1151.